بسم الله الرحمن الرحيم

SAP Customer Master Ultimate Guide

Essential End User Guide; Customer Mater, Credit Management and Customer Hierarchy

SYED AWAIS RIZVI

PUBLICATIONS

Author: **Syed Awais Rizvi**

Copyright © 2018 Syed Awais Rizvi

All rights reserved.

Paperback Edition

ISBN: 1986292339 ISBN-13: 978-1986292337

Paperback Color Edition

ISBN: 1-942554-10-9 ISBN-13: 978-1-942554-10-3

Kindle Edition

ISBN: 1-942554-11-7 ISBN-13: 978-1-942554-11-0

Disclaimer:

DEDICATION

I dedicate this book to my father Tahir Rizvi, Mother Naima and my wife Sairah for her support.

Improve SAP GUI Skills

- **Why this Book?**

Every year thousands of SAP projects implemented around the world. Millions of dollars are spent on SAP implementation hoping for better performance and productivity. Better productivity only improves when users learn SAP with proficiency. In many projects training not considers critically. Training significantly help project to become productive and successful. SAP R/3 comes with many options and flexibilities. Despite modern training end users struggle with essentials. Getting training on GUI and customer master essentials in detail might not be the highest priority in most of the projects. This book coves some SAP GUI introduction and heavily focused on standard SAP customer master. Many companies customize and configure many different probabilities, so in this book reader will find SAP standard functionality. The main goal of this book is to deliver simple and easy learning from customer master standard functionality. If you want to start learning SAP hands on, then skip the first chapter "Introduction to SAP" and start from the chapter two "SAP Navigation." First chapter about information technology and SAP foundation learning.

Ultimately all of the SAP GUI training, tips and tricks from this book comes down to one thing: How to be proficient in SAP Customer master. Learn to utilize high performances to work on SAP efficiently.

The picture speaks thousands of words, book features with SAP screenshots and mind maps throughout the book to make learning simple and easy.

- **Chapter 1 Introduction to SAP**

Learn what is SAP. Learn simple business and SAP relevant terms. Learn about SAP ERP modules, technology and building blocks. Also, this chapter includes some business terms relevant for learning about customer master. Many topics covered with illustrations and mind maps.

- **Chapter 2 SAP Navigation**

  In this chapter learn about SAP ERP GUI basics. This chapter cover brief information about SAP GUI and basics how to use some basics features.

- **Chapter 3 Customer Master**

  Learn customer master general and detail overview. Learn about customer master view. This chapter cover information about most used fields in customer master. Learn how to create, change and view customer. This chapter also covers mass update transaction for customer master.

- **Chapter 4 Customer Credit Master**

  Credit master used for defining customer credit limit. Learn how to setup credit master. Learn about credit control area and how it reflect in customer master.

- **Chapter 5 Customer Hierarchy**

  In this learn about customer hierarchy, how to view and create customer hierarchy.

Who is this book for? Who can use this Book?

- End Users
- Consultants
- Business Analysts
- Managers
- Anyone who want to Learn SAP Customer Master
- SAP ABAPER (Programmer).

Contents

Improve SAP GUI Skills v

CHAPTER 1 12

Introduction to SAP 12

Introduction to SAP: 13
SAP Three Tire System: 13
Application Server: 15
Presentation: 15
Database Server: 16
SAP Netweaver: 16
S/4 HANA 17
SAP Modules: 17
SAP FICO: 18
SAP Sales and Distribution: 19
Best Practices: 19
SAP Configuration: 20
Project: 20
Agile Cycle: 21
Project Issue / Opportunity Management: 21
Issue Log: 21
Project Risk Management: 22
PMO: 22
Project complete life cycle: 23
Enterprise: 24
ECC: 24
EHP: 24
System Landscape: 25
Development System: 25
Quality System: 25
Production System: 26
ABAP: 26
ALV: 26
Internal Number Range: 28
External number range: 28
Data in SAP: 28
Master Data: 28
Transactional Data 29
AR (Account Receivable) and AP (Account Payment): 29

Accrual and cash Basis Accounting: 29
Workflow 29
Use case: 30
General Ledger Accounting: 31
T-Account: 31
Journal entry: 32
Credit 32
Debit 32
Credit and Debit memo 33
SAP Consultant: 33
"Z" and "Y" customization: 33
SAP User Access: 33

CHAPTER 2 ... 35

SAP Navigation ... 35
SAP GUI: 36
SAP GUI Setup: 37
SAP Easy Access Menu: 38
T-code: 39
Tips to remember T-code: 40
T-code Bar: 40
Transaction Code Short Cuts: 41
SAP Copy Paste: 42
Easy Access Menu buttons and shortcuts: 43
SAP Messages T 45
SAP Massage Type 46

CHAPTER 3 ... 48

Customer Master Data ... 48
Master Data Introduction: 49
Enterprise Structure: 49
Company: 50
Company Code: 50
Credit Control Area: 51
Sales Organization: 52
Distribution Channel: 52
Division: 52
Sales Area: 52
Customer Master: 53

General Data 54
Company Code Data 57
Sales Area Data 59
Customer Master Partner Functions: 61
Sold to: 63
Bill to: 63
Ship to Partner function: 63
Payer: 63
Multiple Partner Information: 64
Contact Person partner function: 64
Additional Partner Functions: 65
One Time Customer: 65
Common Distribution Channel: 65
Common Division: 65
Customer Master T-codes: 66
How to Create Customer Master: 68
General Data View: 69
Sales Area View: 76
Company Code View 80
Additional Information 83
Customer Reports: 86
Blocka and Unblock Customer 86
Customer Deletion: 87

CHAPTER 4 89

Customer Credit Management 89
Credit Control Area: 90
Credit Management: 90
What is Customer Credit Exposure: 90
Types of credit check: 90
Simple Credit Check: 91
Automatic credit check: 91
Static Credit Check: 92
Dynamic Credit check: 92
Credit Master (FD32) 92
Credit Control Data: Status 96
Customer: Payment History 96
Customer credit block: 97

CHAPTER 5 98

Customer Hierarchy **98**
Customer Hierarchy: 99
Customer Hierarchy for Rebate: 100
How to Create Customer hierarchy: 100
Display Customer hierarchy: 104
Index: 105

ABOUT THE AUTHOR **107**

ACKNOWLEDGMENTS

الحمد لله ربّ العالمين

The most forgiving person is one who forgives in spite of his ability to punish.

Saying of Imam Hussain (a.s)

I would like to thank my mother and father for the support. My book would not have been possible without amazing support of my wife Sairah. I would like to thank my family for the support and love. I would like to thank my brothers Imon Rizvi for always encouraging words. I would like to thank my beloved teacher Ustad Sibtay Jaffer for his kind guidance and devoted support. Ustad Sibtay Jaffer is a living example for all of his students and community for his humbleness, kindness and intellectual noble contributions.

Chapter 1

Introduction to SAP

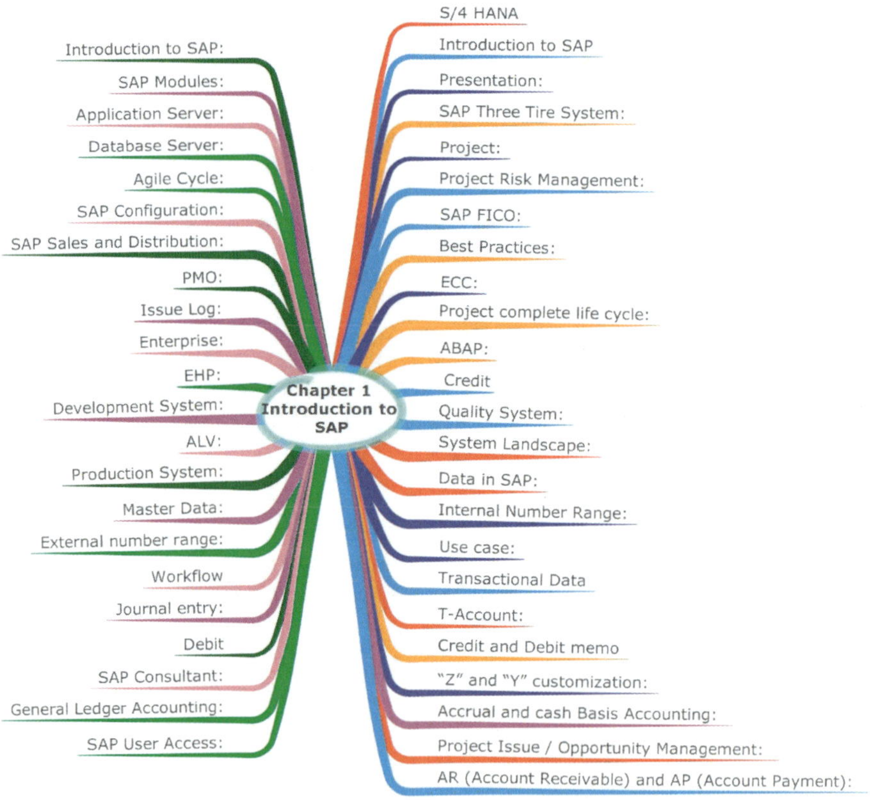

Introduction to SAP:

SAP AG is a name of German Software Company, commonly known for ERP application with many enterprise products. SAP stands for Systems, Applications and Products in data processing. In any business three departments are very important, finance, logistics and human resource. SAP provided modules under accounting, logistics and human resources. Many models are available for accounting, logistics or human resources. SAP modules designed to represent independent business departments. One of the key benefits of SAP ERP modules is that they are, integrated and centralize with business functions.

SAP modules offer best practices and "industry standards."

IS-Retail
IS-Oil and Gas
IS-Auto

SAP Three Tire System:

ERP industry constantly changing with new technology for performance. Currently SAP new ERP application called S/4 HANA. The previous version of SAP ERP's called "SAP ECC," that stands for ERP Central Component. SAP ERP represented by three-tier based system with each tier representing each section of the software application.

- **Application (Application Server)**

- **Presentation (Computer, mobile, web, etc.)**
- **Database (Database server)**

Subsequent Figure Present the three-tier system.

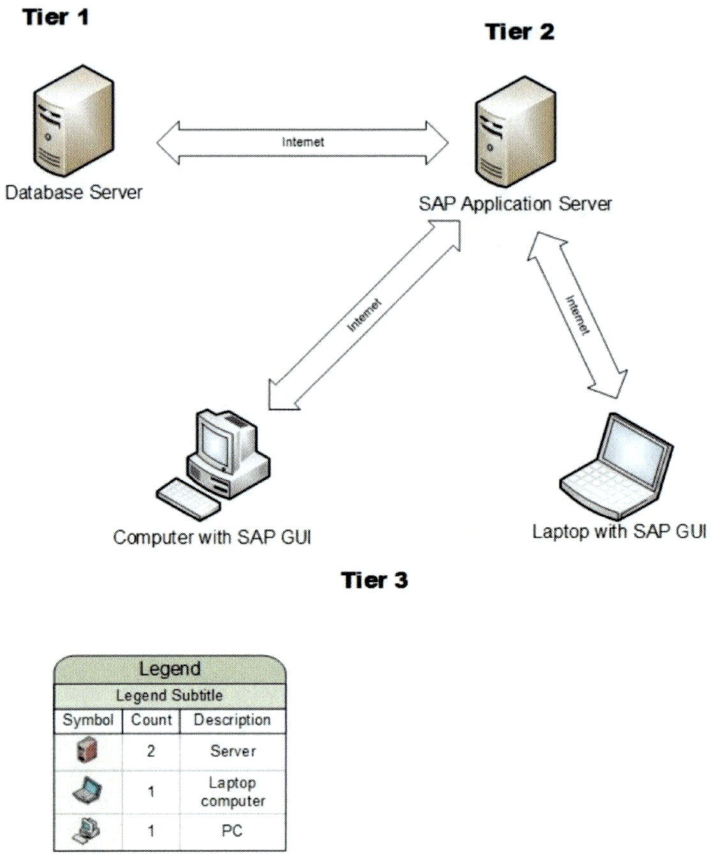

Figure 1

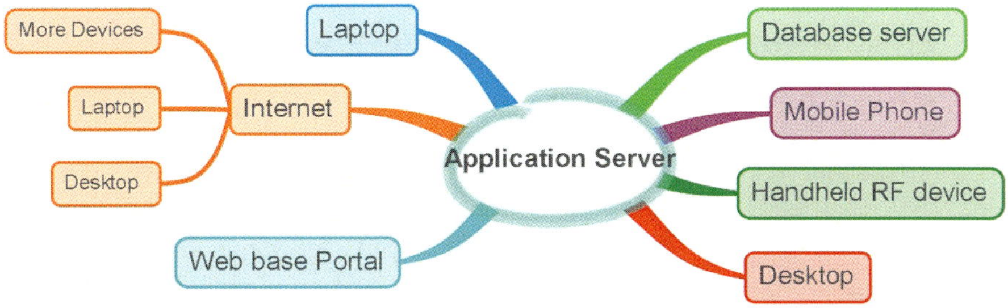

Figure 2

Application Server:

SAP GUI interact with SAP application server to access SAP data base. SAP application server is a center point to access database server and to serve SAP GUI. SAP application server can be connected with different types of databases. SAP application server name used in SAP GUI connection.

Presentation:

In order to access SAP, we need a software installed on a computer called SAP GUI. With SAP GUI we can access SAP R/3 application. GUI is a SAP presentation layer to present SAP application on a computer. SAP GUI also come with upgrade for example version 7.4 or 7.2.

Database Server:

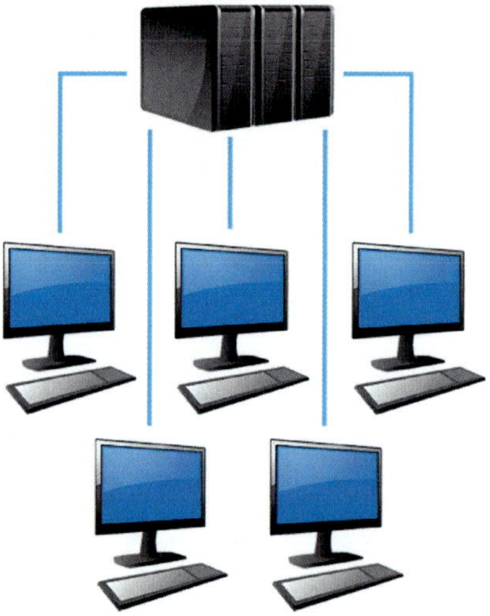

Database represents a collection of tables. SAP database reside on a separate server called SAP database server. SAP database server is a one component of a three layer SAP ECC system.

SAP Netweaver:

SAP Netweaver is a technology platform, which integrates SAP business suite and non-SAP application for integration, portal, security and services.

Trick to remember what Netweaver do, Net = Internet and Weaver which integrates or put together applications to communicates.

S/4 HANA

S/4 HANA stands for SAP business suite build with in memory computing, where database stays in memory. One of key reason SAP HANA was developed is to improve performance and reduce database footprint. SAP HANA offers in memory computing where application reside on a memory with some part of the database also resides on a memory too. With SAP innovation SAP application server and SAP Database server reside on memory. SAP HANA also used a column base store for improved performance.

For more information on SAP HANA check free courses offered by SAP, https://open.sap.com/.

SAP Modules:

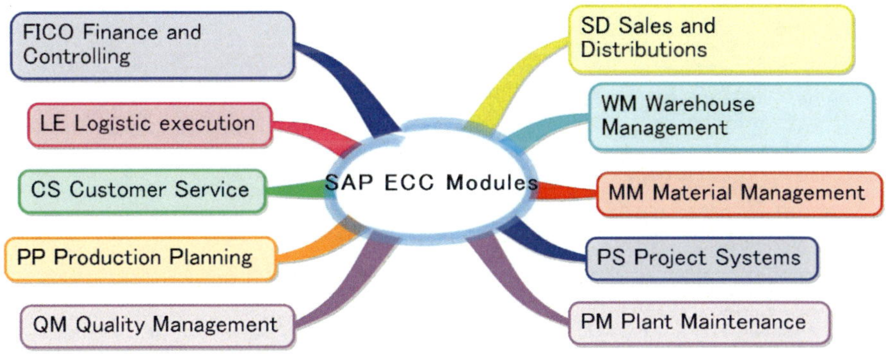

Figure 3

Any business consists of many departments, SAP ERP solution divided into many modules for the different department to accommodate business functions. Most businesses has three main departments:

- Accounting
- Human resource
- Logistics

Business departments can be divided into many more sub divisions. The sub division of these main unites of business are represented as modules in SAP.

SAP FICO:

FICO stands for finance and controlling. SAP FI and CO represent two different finance modules which goes together hand to hand. Figure 4 show some of the accounting modules in SAP.

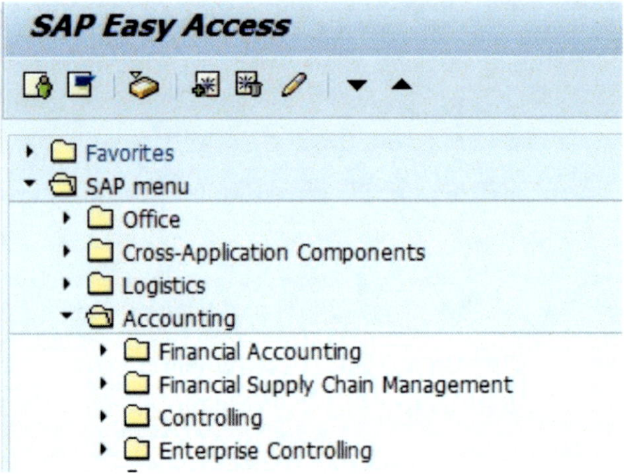

Figure 4

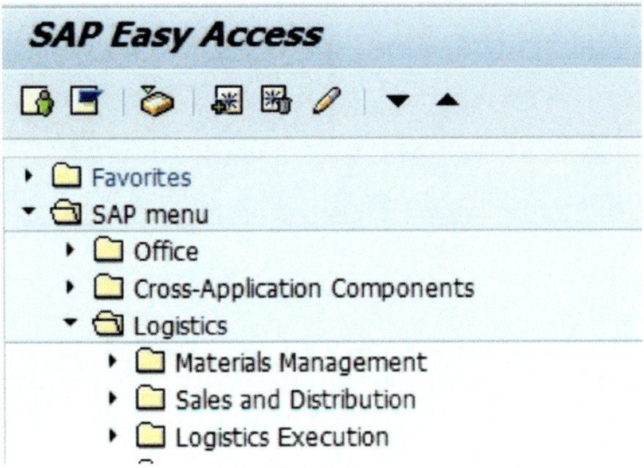

SAP Sales and Distribution:

SAP Sales and distribution feature functionalities for order to cash cycle. SAP SD offer functions for sales, pricing, and billing. SAP SD integrates with FICO, MM, PP and many more modules to accommodate the process.

Best Practices:

What are best practices? Best practices represented the industry's standard. Best practice given the industry the highest value after international standards of ISO 9000. SAP process and function are based on the best practice.

SAP Best practice represented by out of box functionalities. Industry best practice can help companies to stream line their processes.

Tips:

- Best practice improve business process
- Best practice also provide industry standards
- Best practices do not require ABAP programing

SAP Configuration:

SAP out of the box requires preparation configuration setup for master and transactional setups. Customization in SAP called IMG. IMG stands for Implementation Guide.

To customize one can use T-code: SPRO

- Configuration perform by analyst, consultants, and configurators.

Project:

Any strategy for a task with beginning and end can be called project. The project cannot be completed without consideration of project plan, project scope, and resources. Many methodologies are available for project implementations.

Agile Cycle:

What represent a project cycle? “Agile” mythology feature small incremental cycles. Each Cycle features deliverables and a set of activities to consider and complete. Project cycle represents a developing and completing portion of functionality.

Project Issue / Opportunity Management:

Every issue is an opportunity for correction. Issues are part of many project thought out any software implementation. Many companies maintain issue and risk log to use them as opportunities to improve.

Issue Log:

Keeping an issue log is ongoing process to track bugs in a software before and after implementation. Issues are logged based on system performance, user complaints, testing, etc. Many tools are able to utilize and manage issue logs.

Project Risk Management:

Risk is part of our life, starting by driving on a road to taking stairs, etc. Risks can be defined as predictions of issues in future. Risk expected to be identifying in any stage of the project. The biggest risk exist when project managers, stakeholders, and team members ignore potential risks. Risk also supposed to be kept in a risk log and tracked to avoid future issues.

PMO:

PMO stands for Project Management Office or officer. Project managers are experienced individuals who look after the project.

Project complete life cycle:

Any project that is completed from start to finish is considered a full lifecycle.

ERP

Representation of ERP in mind map.

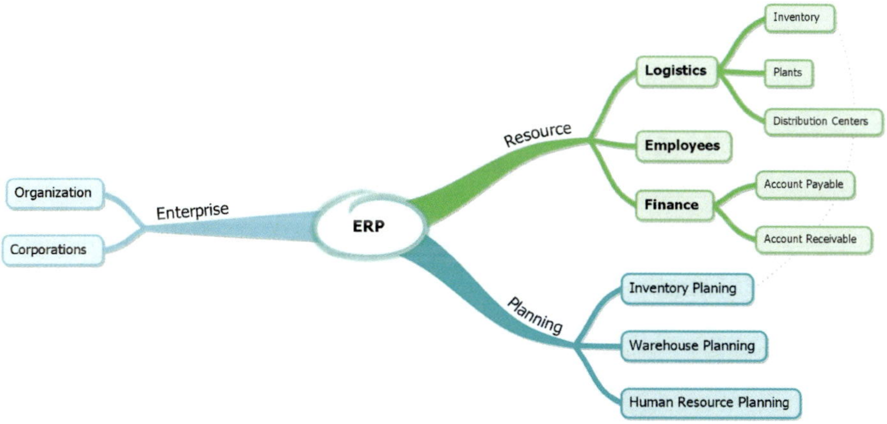

Figure E786

ERP Stands for Enterprise Resource Planning. Few of the ERP functions are defined in the figure E786 and show how enterprise resource planning works. Many business departments are managed by the organization, thus the ERP software becomes a necessity that able to handle multiple departments and resources centrally.

Enterprise:

Enterprise represents a business or organization. Any big organization with many departments can be called as enterprise.

ECC:

ECC stands for ERP central Component. ECC abbreviation employ by SAP to identify its new release of SAP. Usually ECC term practice for SAP version ERP 5.0 ECC OR SAPERP 6.0.

EHP:

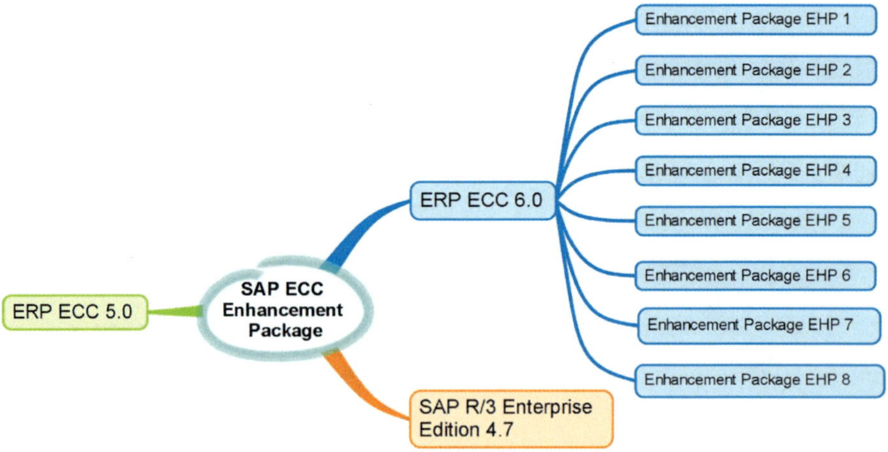

Figure E787

EHP stands for ECC Enhancement Pack. Each version of SAP follow with many enhancement packs figure E787. Enhancement pack provides new features and upgrades to the latest version of SAP ERP ECC.

The latest version of SAP ERP ECC 6.0 enhancement pack "**SAP ECC**

6.0 EHP 8"

System Landscape:

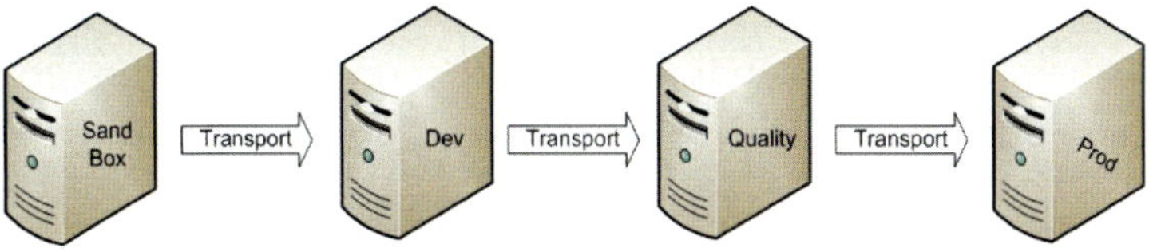

System Landscape

We use system landscape to develop identical objects to prepare it in deployment system, test it, in test system and finally copy the finish product to production system. System landscapes mostly consist of three or more identical environments for project life cycle. In a project, we develop functions in a "development system" and then it gets copy to "quality server" for testing. After the successful testing, it will be transported to the "production system".

In general, system landscapes consist of three system environments:

- Development
- Quality
- Production

Development System:

Development system utilizes for system configuration and custom developments. Many projects also maintain sand box with addition to development system.

Quality System:

Quality system used when project team needs to test the changes. Quality system also utilized for user acceptance testing, regression testing, etc.

Production System:

Any system which called a system of the records or any system that is used for real-time transactions is call production system. Many companies start using SAP live system after the project cycle is completed.

ABAP:

ABAP stands for Advance Business Application Programming. ABAP is SAP language for SAP system enhancements. ABAP Programming is used for new enhancements, transactions, report, etc. ABAP is SAP language for development.

T-codes:

- ABAPHELP
- ABAPDOCU

ALV:

Most of SAP reports features in ALV, ALV stands for ABAP list viewer. With ALV user has option to select different variations and selection to slice and dice the data. With this, users able to hide, display, or suppress fields or control header and item level information into the report. ALV is a very flexible tool for reports.

Database:

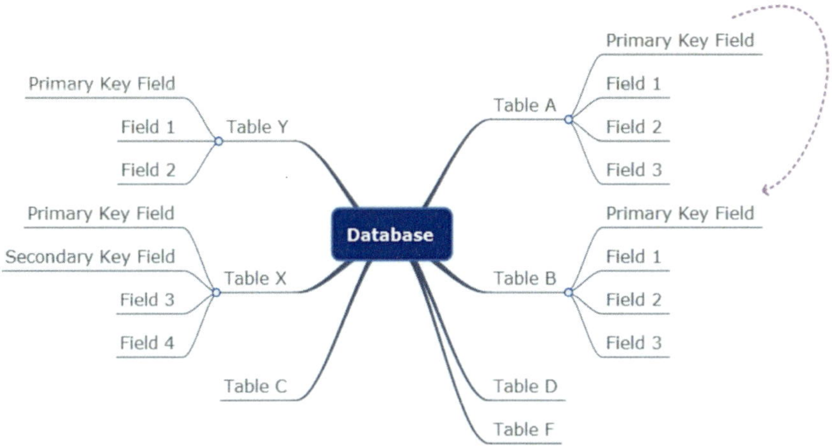

Logical collection of tables can be called tables. The table consists of rows and columns, with reference to database. Database servers maintain databases.

Number Range:

Number range is an identifier which controls document number, sequencing, limit of numbers and manual numbers. Mostly number range controls the number of transactional data. Number range represents a SAP configuration for transactional or master data. Series of number ranges utilized differently for different transactions. In SAP two types of number ranges exist:

1. **Internal Number Range (Automatics)**
2. **External Number Range (non-automatic)**

Internal number range automatically selected by a system, and external number range will not assign a number to new transaction.

Internal Number Range:

Internal number range used where we want system to automatically assign next number to master data or transactional data.

For example, if the customer is created with internal number range then, system automatically selects a next available number from internal number range.

External number range:

Internal number range used where we want to assign number for master data or transactional data manually.

Example of Internal Number range:

If the customer created with external number range, then system will not assign new number instead system will give error massage to enter the number for new customer.

Data in SAP:

SAP feature two types of data.

1. Master Data
2. Transactional Data

Master Data:

The data that hardly changes and utilized in transactions. The example of master data in SAP are:

- Customer master
- Vendor Master
- Pricing Master

Transactional Data

Data that changes often called a transactional data. Transactional data always based on a master data with variations of transactions. The sales document, delivery and billing document represents the good examples of transactional data.

AR (Account Receivable) and AP (Account Payment):

AR refers to account receivable, which is utilized in the revenue for the sales income.

Accrual and cash Basis Accounting:

In accounting, revenue is calculated on the basis of either cash or accrual. Accrual mean added up and keeping track of it. On the accrual basis of accounting the amount is tracked and eventually it is posted for accounting purposes. Cash basis accounting is posted as soon as the transaction is processed in the system or accounting.

Workflow:

Workflow is a system of work that goes through business approvals and administration approvals. SAP Workflow feature a process of approvals in system. Also, in SAP, workflow is part of RECIFW that is counted toward system change, other than the standard functionality of SAP ERP.

Use case:

Use case is a pictorial representation of the process. Use case helps visual process flow for better understanding. The use case features Actors in stick figures interacting with system define in the middle. Use case is created in requirement gathering and documentation for the project.

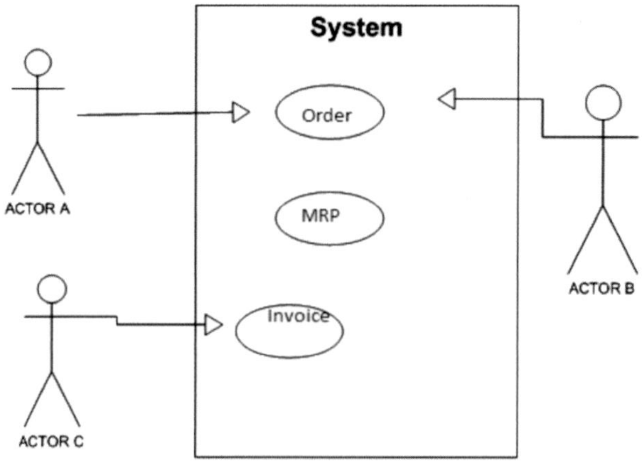

General Ledger Accounting:

The general ledger accounting is an account for all business transactions. GL is utilized for profit, loss report and financial calculation, etc. It is very important for businesses to keep track of transaction for legal and accountability. The SAP feature general ledger accounting is integrated with all of the modules to keep track of all financial transactions.

T-Account:

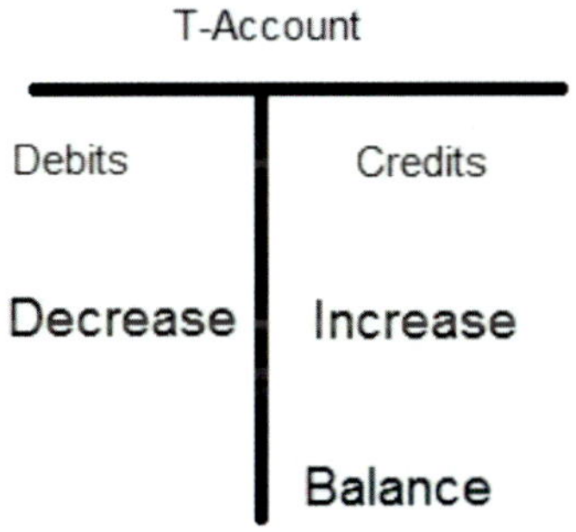

T-account is utilized in accounting with journal entries. On the left side of the T-account is debit and on the right side is credit. In the figure above, we able to see that the left side is the debit and that the right side is credit. At the end of the T-account, we able to see balance from both sides of transactions and keep track of journal leader balance with sub T-accounts.

Journal entry:

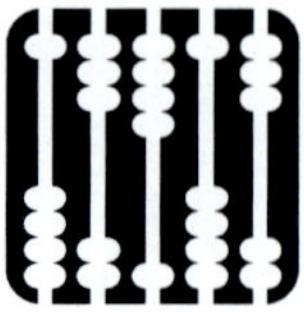

In T-accounting each transaction is entered either on debit or credit, this is what is called a journal entry.

Credit

Credit means an increase in amount or gain. Credit refers to entry in accounting when balance increases. When we over pay our bill then, we will receive a credit balance transfer back.

Debit

In accounting, debit refers to the decrease in the account. For example, debit means to pay out something so it decreased amount is transfer out of the balance.

Credit and Debit memo

Credit and Debit memo are an invoice document in SAP.

SME:

SME stands for Subject Mater Expert. Subject matter expert is a title given to technology or business related knowledge.

SAP Consultant:

SAP Consultant is a title for the role in which his/her responsibilities fall into the project implementation or support role.

"Z" and "Y" customization:

SAP recommends customization to start with "Z" and "Y". When customization start with "Z" or "Y" it will not be over written on upgrades.

SAP User Access:

SAP users are defined with roles and access for transactions. Different users have different access for transactions to create, change and display. These accesses are created so segregation of functions can be defined as per authorization and business process.

Notes

Chapter 2

SAP Navigation

SAP GUI:

GUI stands for graphical user interface. SAP GUI is a SAP software which installs on a computer. Most companies uses windows operating system to install SAP GUI. There is also a GUI version available for apple systems. GUI software is a shell, to access SAP ECC system. SAP GUI requires configuration with address of SAP application server to be connected. SAP GUI features options for ECC, SCM, CRM and other components to access.

GUI Installation steps:

Screenshots figure G786 display, steps to install SAP GUI from SAP install file.

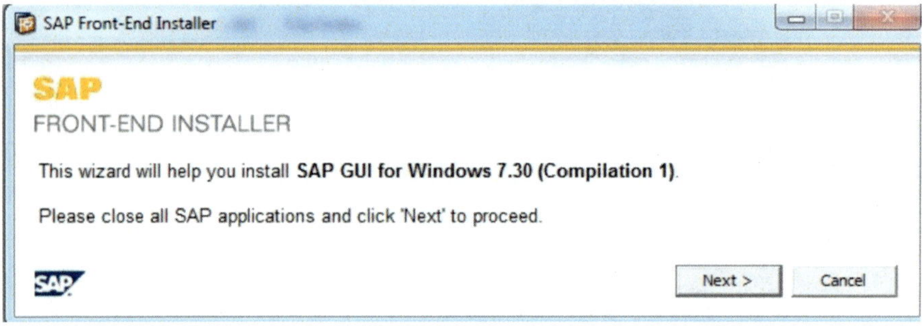

SAP Front-End Installer
SAP
FRONT-END INSTALLER
This wizard will help you install SAP GUI for Windows 7.30 (Compilation 1).
Please close all SAP applications and click 'Next' to proceed.
Next >
Cancel

Figure G786

Select the first option from the screenshot figure G787 to enable ECC access. From same process user can install other SAP GUI components as display figure G787.

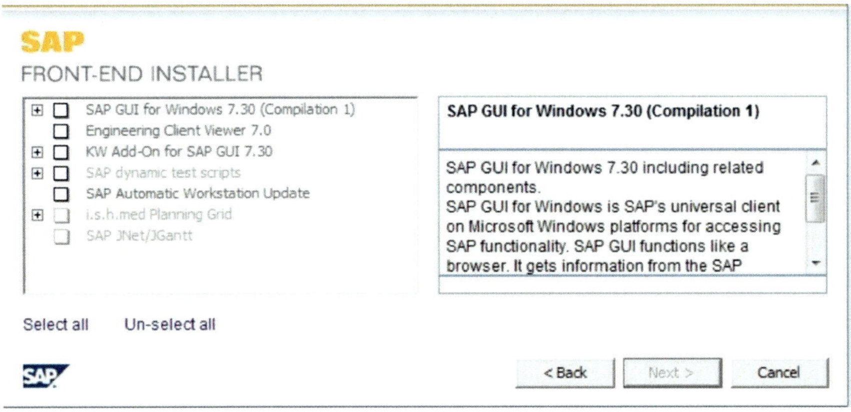

Figure G787

After SAP completely Installed on a computer, SAP GUI shortcut will appear on desktop or programs folder figure G788.

Figure G788

SAP GUI Setup:

GUI is a tool to access SAP ECC server remotely. SAP GUI requires SAP ECC credentials to access SAP application. To setup GUI access open GUI application from the desktop icon and click on new connection.

Screenshot of how to setup SAP new connection.

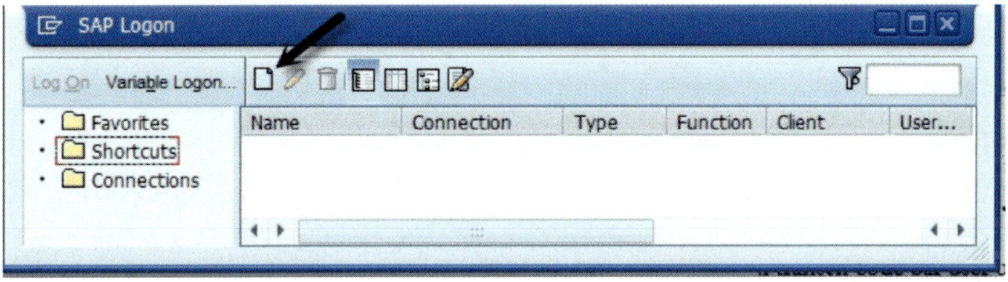

Figure G789

To setup new access, follow arrow from above screenshot figure G789. Each organization maintains their own credentials for SAP ECC access.

Screenshot figure G790 of SAP credentials setup.

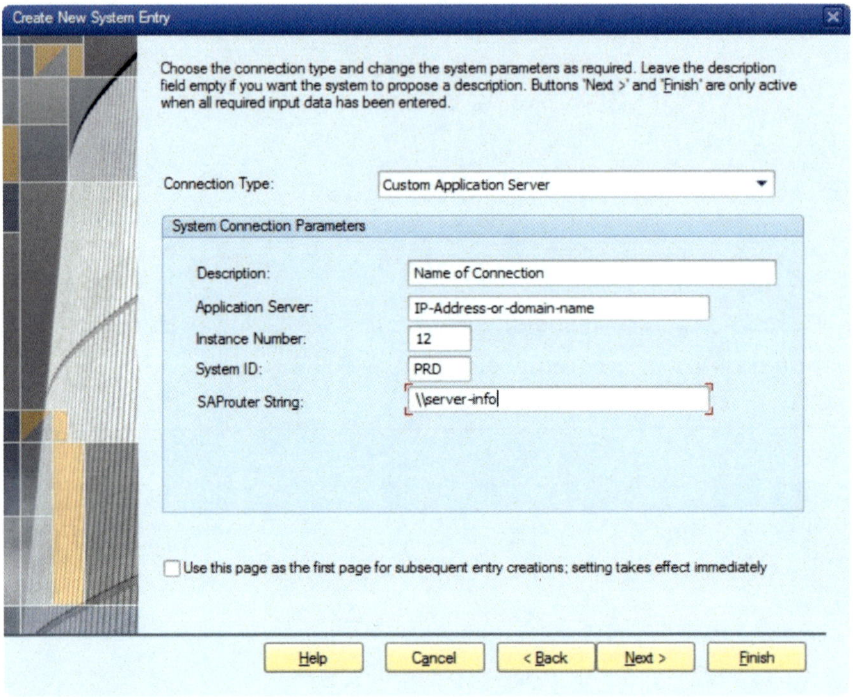
Create New System Entry
Choose the connection type and change the system parameters as required. Leave the description field empty if you want the system to propose a description. Buttons 'Next >' and 'Finish' are only active when all required input data has been entered.
Connection Type:
Custom Application Server
System Connection Parameters
Description:
Name of Connection
Application Server:
IP-Address-or-domain-name
Instance Number:
12
System ID:
PRD
SAProuter String:
\\server-info
Use this page as the first page for subsequent entry creations; setting takes effect immediately
Help
Cancel
< Back
Next >
Finish

Figure G790

In above screenshot user enters credentials including: description, application server information, instance number, system ID and SAProuter String. Consider the information provided by SAP security team or system admin for SAP GUI. Each company setup SAP GUI differently.

SAP Easy Access Menu:

First SAP screen initial screen called SAP easy access menu screenshot figure G791. SAP Easy access menu has many different options for SAP interface. In SAP GUI one can open up to six sessions from single log in.

- The easy access menu easily customizable with GUI options.
- Most SAP easy access menu allow up to six separate sessions open

at same time.

- The easy access menu has a transaction code bar for transactions.
- SAP Easy access menu feature favorites shortcuts to transactions.

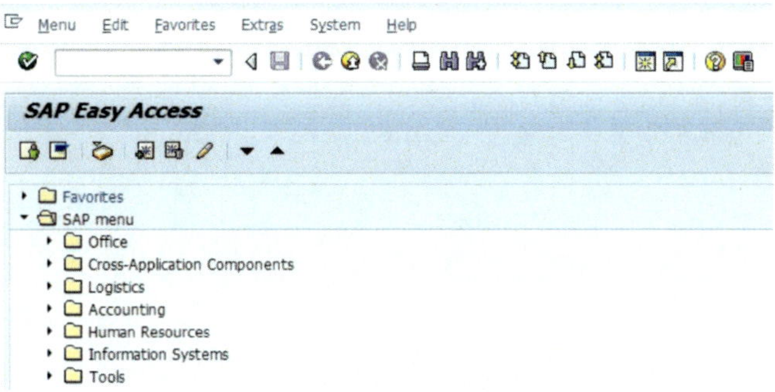

Figure G791

T-code:

T-code stands for transaction code. T-code is a short cut to the transaction in SAP to execute the transaction, the easy access menu features a transaction code bar, as seen in the screenshot figure G792. In this t-code bar user enters the t-codes to be executed from SAP GUI.

Example: VA01 is a transaction code to create a sales order.

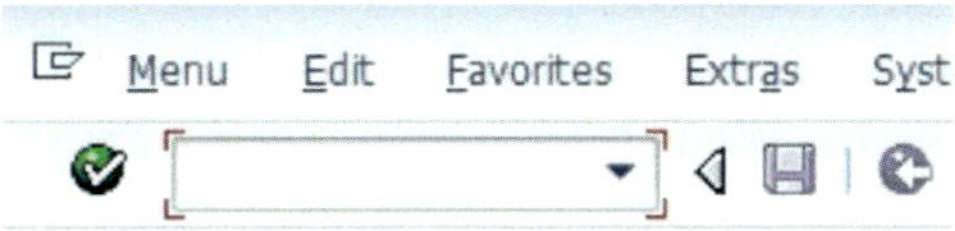

Figure G792

Tips to remember T-code:

Here are some of the tips to remember transaction code reference to alphabets.

Character	Description
N	Number
V	Sales
F	Billing
M	Material Master
01	Create
02	Changes
03	Display
05	Report

For sales related MENU use t-code: **VA00**

T-code Bar:

Figure G793

T-code bar represent place where user enters the transaction code screenshot figure G793. Alternatively, user can use folder structure to execute the transaction.

Instructions:

Click on t-code bar and enter the transaction code, there is also small triangle on the left side of T-code bar to hide and display screenshot figure G793.

Transaction Code Short Cuts:

I would highly recommend remembering the shortcuts to improve productivity. From transaction code bar user uses following short cuts to process the transactions.

T-code	Description	shortcut
/o	Open New Session	Ctrl + O
/n	To end the current transaction	
/i	To delete the current session	Alt + F4
/nend	To log off with saving	
/nex	Exit without saving	

Tips: Most used shortcut is "/n" to end current session. User use next T-code after "/n" ending current session. For example, first user reviews the customer master and from same screen user would like to view sales order.

/n(t-code)

Example:

/NVA03 (t-codes are not case sensitive)

Use shortcut to end current session and enter the next t-code after the shortcut:

/*(T-code)

when "/*" is used it will skip over the first screen to enter values and press enter. It can be useful with combination of the parameter and last entry from transaction. For example, if user saved a sales order then use /*VA02 to go into change sales order directly.

SAP Copy Paste:

In SAP copy, paste function work with command "Ctrl + Y", and it display plus sign to text to be selected. User can copy text by scrolling over and select "Ctrl + C". Text paste with "Ctrl + V".

Select Text	=	Ctrl + Y	" + "
Copy	=	Ctrl + C	
Past	=	Ctrl + V	

Easy Access Menu buttons and shortcuts:

Button	Description	Shortcut
	Enter	
	Command Field for T-codes the triangle close the command field	
	Save	ctrl + S
	Back	F3
	Log Off (from current session)	Shift + F3
	Cancel	F12
	Print	Ctrl + P
	Find	Ctrl + F
	Find Next	Ctrl + G

Button	Description	Shortcut
	First Page	Ctrl + page up
	Page up	
	Page Down	
	Last Page	Ctrl + pg den
	New Session	Ctrl + N
	Create shortcut	
	Help	F1
	Customize Local Layout (change Color, themes, font size, etc.)	
	Add to Favorites	Ctrl + shift + F6
	Delete Favorite	Shift + F12
	Change Favorite	Ctrl + shift + F3

SAP Messages Types:

SAP error messages are defined in different categories. Some errors are not able to bypass. If an error which is normally red comes on, it means it's a hard error and cannot sustain to ignore. Not all errors are hard errors, these errors are called soft errors; These warning error color is yellow and it able to ignore, however the user will see warnings. In the event that the transaction system issues a message, it means that the status of transaction changed by the user. In SAP, messages are defined in different categories, with their own message types. Each process features a message type in SAP. It gives a status to the user that results in success and failure:

1. **Warring**
2. **Error**
3. **Exit**
4. **Success**

Each process features a message type in SAP. It gives a status to the user that results in success and failure.

SAP Massage Type

Message Type	Icon	Description
Information		The message type is for information purposes, by clicking the icon it will open a new window with information.
Warning:		It feature warned you on the next step. It will be able to correct before the warning is ignored. (The user able to ignore it by pressing enter) The warning may appear more than once based on transactions. It appears on left bottom of the screen.
Hard Error		Message gives a hard stop. Unless the correction is made, it will stay as error and will not process.
Exit		Message exits the trisections and gives a short dump or stop the transaction.
Success		Success message with document number or if this transaction is successful this will appear. It appears on left bottom of the screen.

Notes

Chapter 3

Customer Master Data

Figure CM786

Chapter Summary:

The chapter divided into two sections first section contain brief information and second section is on hands on with screenshots; Step by step guide explained with screenshots. Scope of chapter is on guide limited to SAP standard functions. Each company use their own specific, company code, sales areas, please consider those as per the unique systems.

Master Data Introduction:

The short description of master data is that "Master data hardly changes." Master data is the means of transactions, for example the customer and products (material) utilized for sales order creation. Master Data is required to create transactions like sales orders, delivery, invoice, etc. SAP Sales and Distribution master data elements are customer Master, Material Master and Pricing Records. The master data are based on a group of tables for each master data. To represent one master data, each table represents a unique view of the master data. In SAP Sales and Distribution Customer master, material master and condition records are important master data.

Enterprise Structure:

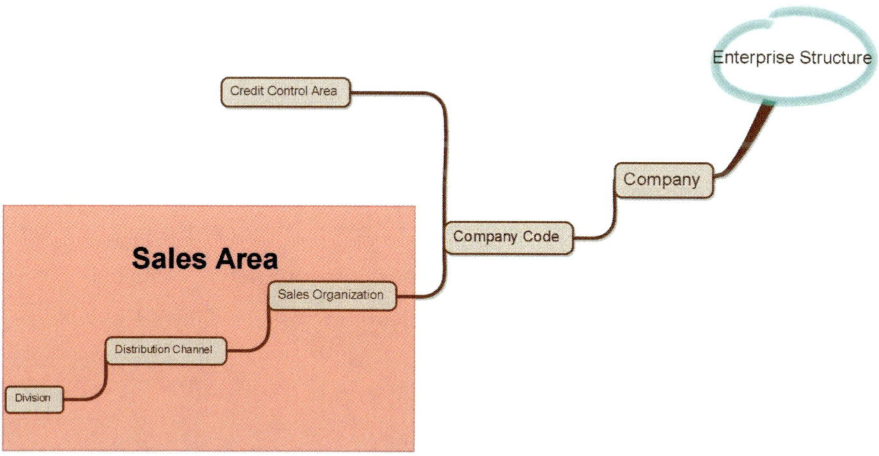

Figure CM787

Enterprise structure is the basis of master data setup in SAP. In SAP we setup enterprise structure to identify company, sales organization and sales channels etc. Enterprise structure can be designed as per SAP defined enterprise elements. For customer master we need to understand company code, credit control area, sales organization, distribution center and division. All the enterprise structure elements are defined in detail. Minimum enterprise structure result less master data. For example, if company decided to create many sales areas then each sales area need to have additional sales area view for customer master.

Company:

Company represents a business, legal entity. In SAP Company defined with four numbers of letters, each company able to assign multiple company codes to it. In SAP company number created with alpha or numeric characters. Company's creation in SAP is a responsibility of FICO consultant.

Example: Company "XYZ" able to have one company code from the United States and one company code from Canada. Each company code will be the legal entity formed in that country and feature separate transactions specific to that company's code.

Company Code:

Company code represents the financial and organizational unit in SAP. Company code represents the legal entity. Company code customization. Each company code maintained with address, currency, language etc. Every company code result in customer master as company code view. One customer defined in one company code and same customer can be created for another company code, but company code data will be different for each company code.

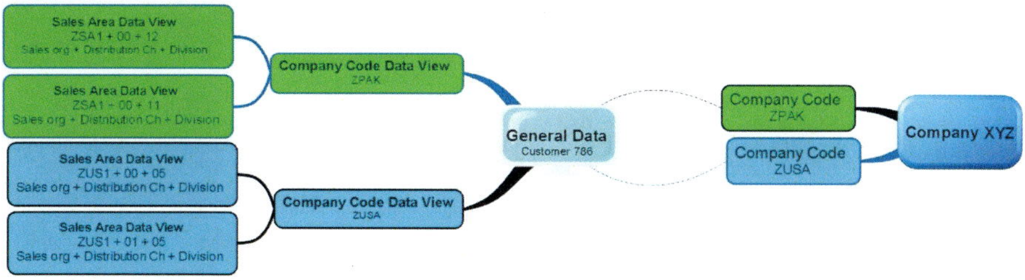

Figure CC786

Customer from figure CC786 shows that customer will be linked to two company codes.

Customer record in system will be:

- 786 + ZPAK
- 786 + ZUSA

So customer 786 is the same but the company code data is different data as per company code view.

Credit Control Area:

Credit control area defines how customer's credit controls are setup for credit related transactions. Control area customizations able to manage independently or centrally managed. Credit control area controls the customer's credit functionality. The credit control area should have the same currency as company's code. Each company's code with one credit control assigned to it, but credit control able to have many company codes assigned to it. The credit control area also able to assign to multiple company codes. The credit control area is utilized in customer credit master creation. Credit Control Area customization is the responsibility of the SAP FI and SD modules area.

Sales Organization:

Sales organization is an organizational unit that is responsible for sales activity. This organizational element is represented in SAP by the enterprise element of sales organization. Sales organization able to define with the alphabet and numeric values. Sales organizations are only assigned to one company code. The one company code able to have multiple sales organizations assigned to it. Sales organizations able to define based on the location or business requirements. Sales organization customization comes under the Sales and Distribution consultant.

Distribution Channel:

In the SAP distribution channel represent ways of distribution. Distribution channels are utilized for different means of distributions. Some examples of the distribution channels are: direct sales, online, retail, wholesale, etc. Distribution channels able to assign to multiple sales organizations, also in sales, distribution channels assigned to the plant.

Division:

Division represents the "line of products". For example, company XYZ able to have two different product lines, so that different divisions able to separate them. In SAP, the division is assigned to sales organization. The division able to assign to multiple sales organizations or utilized in the sales area setup. Division utilized in customer and material master.

Sales Area:

Sales area represents a unique combination of sales organization, distribution, and division. The sales area utilized for the master data setup and becomes the basis for the transactions, along with the master data creation. The sales area required for the customer master creation. In the sales area setup, the sales organization assigned with distribution channel and division with unique combinations. Sales and Distribution consultants or analyst configure sales areas for customization.

Each sales area defined as sales view in customer master. If customer defined in five different sales areas, then there will be five different sales views. Each sales view have different view, so each view can be defined with own data relevant to sales area. Figure CC786 is great example for two different sales areas result in different sales view.

Customer Master:

Customer master represents customer information in SAP. Customer master utilized for different business functions. Customer master feature functionality driven from customer master into transactions. SAP Customer master divided into three different views.

1. General Data
2. Company Code Data
3. Sales Data

Customer Master Mind Map

Screenshot of SAP where we can view three views are highlighted.

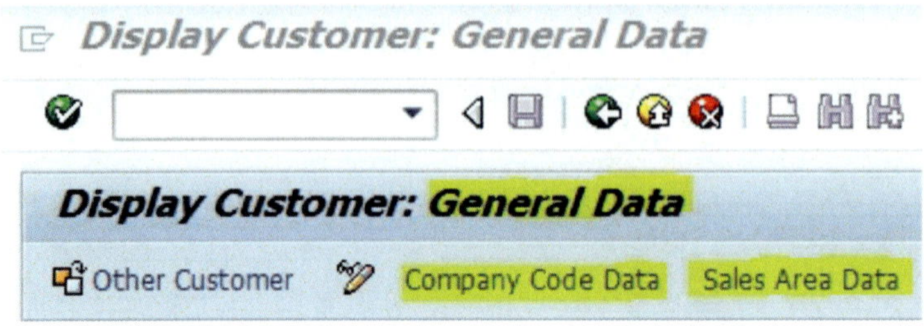

 Figure C12

Every view of customer master have sub tabs where different fields are available to user to view or change. Customer general data from figure C12 highlighted to represent that this view will display general data sub tabs.

Three different views are created to maintain different business sections. This view also relates to functions, or roles. A customer master able to create with two combinations: General data with Company code and data or General data with Sales area Data. The Customer Master also able to maintain centrally with all the views. General data consists of general information such as the name, address, P.O box address, phone number, fax number, and so on. Sales Data consist of billing, shipping, pricing, related information, and partner functions. With master data and Customer Master additional data is also available for control and functionality.

General Data

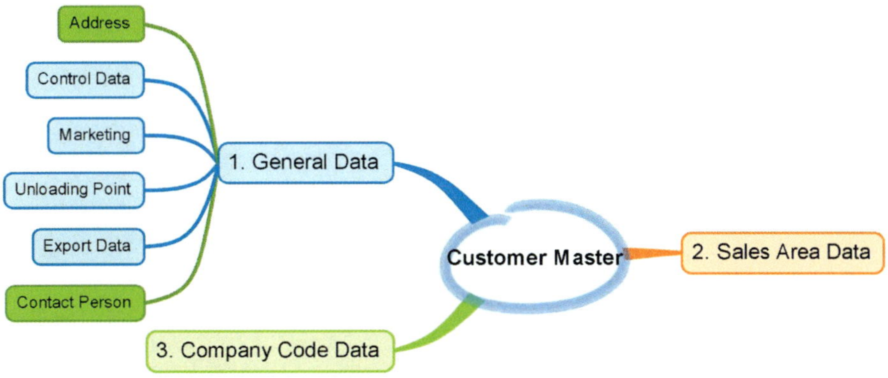

Figure C13

General data consists of the name, address, phone, and fax from the address tabs. With Each tab from the Customer Master General Data feature more detail information from customer Master. Each BOX from mind map represent tab view within general view of customer master. Boxes in green indicate about tab which are used the most, not all the fields of customer master are used generally. Address tab contains name address, tax jurisdiction code etc. Contact person tab contain information about contact person, in this tab we can find one or more contact person, each contact person have their own detail view with the name, designation, address, phone and email etc.

To view customer T-code is utilized XD01

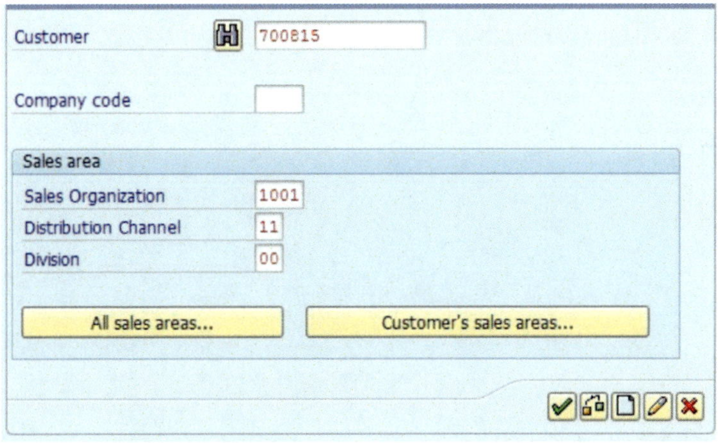

Figure CM788

To view, a user should enter: customer number, company code, and sales area number.

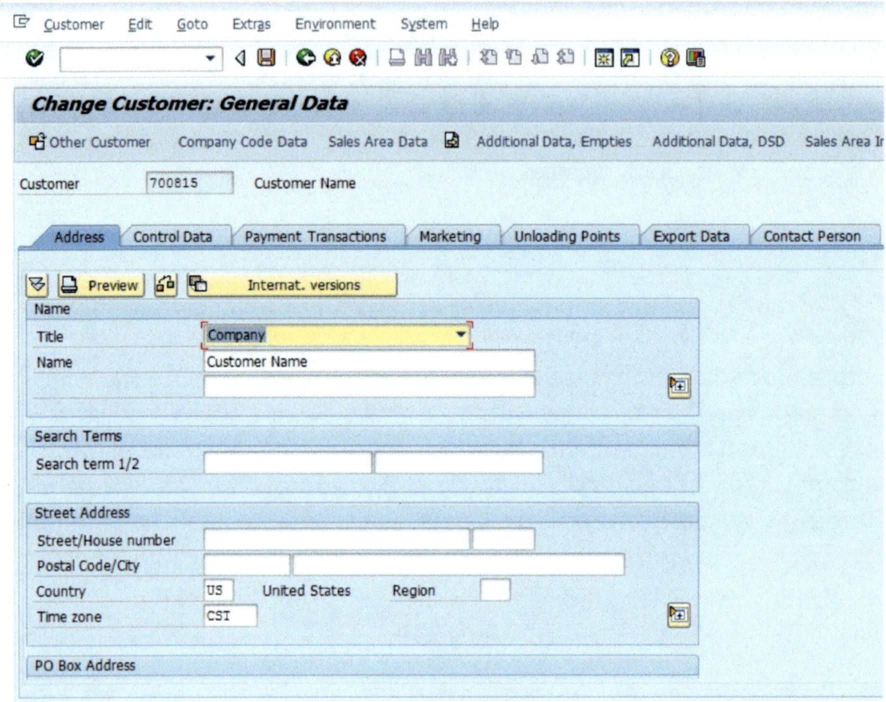

 Figure CM789

Each view feature heading on the top of the page to represent each view

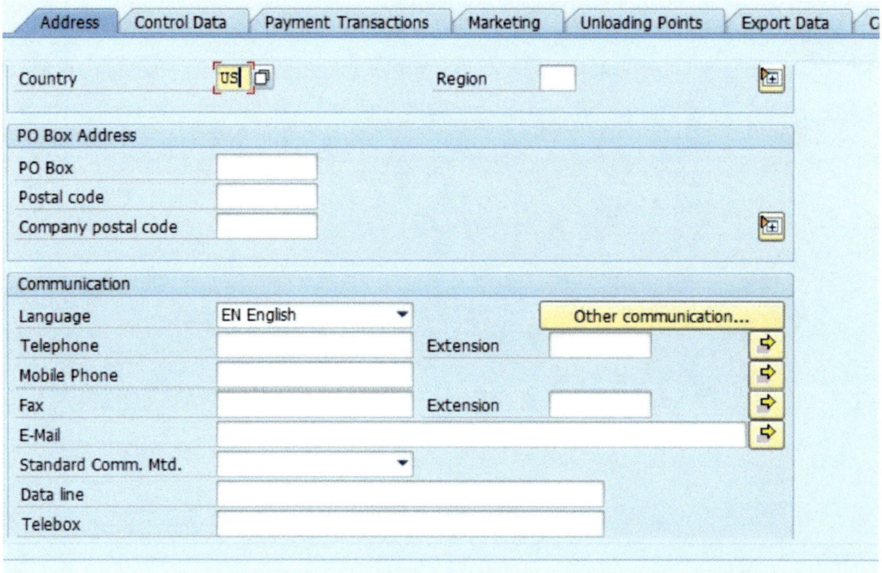

 Figure CM790

Company Code Data

Company code data feature the customer financial related information. Company code view screenshot reference in figure CM792. Customer master company code view feature four tabs for company code relevant data. Each tab contain relevant data to the tab header. Reference screenshot figure CM792 tab view of "Account Management", most important field for this view is "Recon. Account".

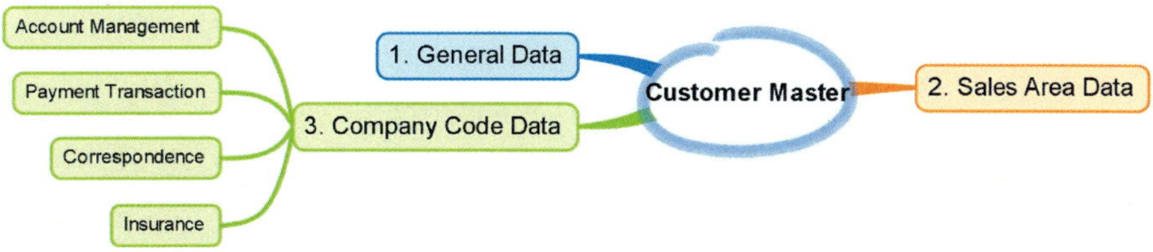

Figure CM791

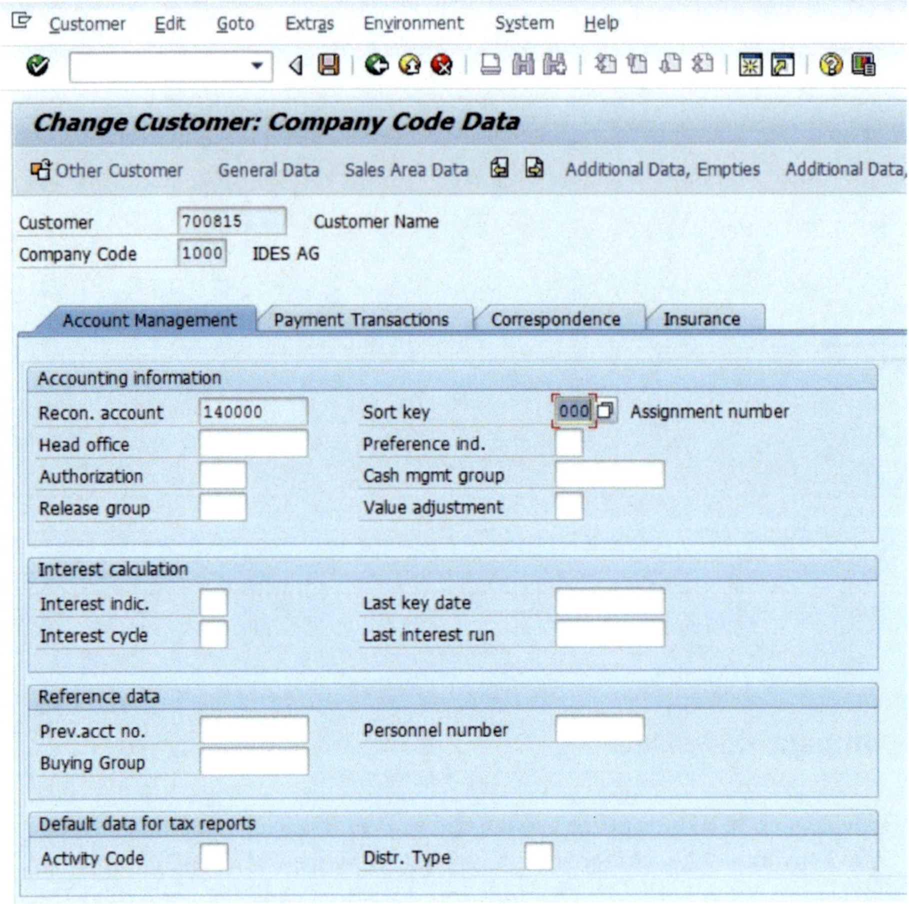

 Figure CM792

Recon. Account:

Reconciliation account automatically post to GL for account raceable when billing document created.

Sales Area Data

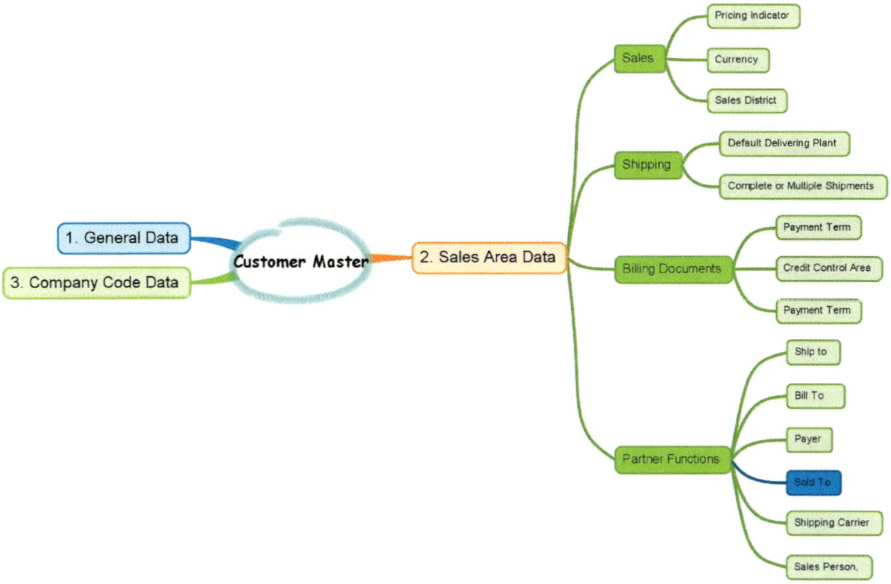

Figure 5SAL

Sales area consists of a unique combination of sales organization, distribution channel, and division. Sales data also feature additional information related to that of the sales area like plant, partner function, shipping and billing information. Customer sales view from figure 5SAL features boxes after sales area data to a tab. Each tab represents different group of fields for customer controls. Each additional sales area contains additional sales views, mind map figure CC786 displays how same customer have different sales area data based on multiple sales area.

To create a customer master three different T-codes are followed.

1. XD01 Centrally with all the views
2. FD01 General and Company Code Data
3. VD01 General and sales area data

XD01 includes all the views to create customer master. VD01 includes sales area and general area views. FD01 includes general data and company code view.

Why three different t-codes to create customer master?

Three different t-codes used for segregation of duty in different departments and authorization regarding customer master.

The following four tabs are sales area view of customer master

Sales Area Data View

Figure CM793

Each Sales Area Data feature many fields.

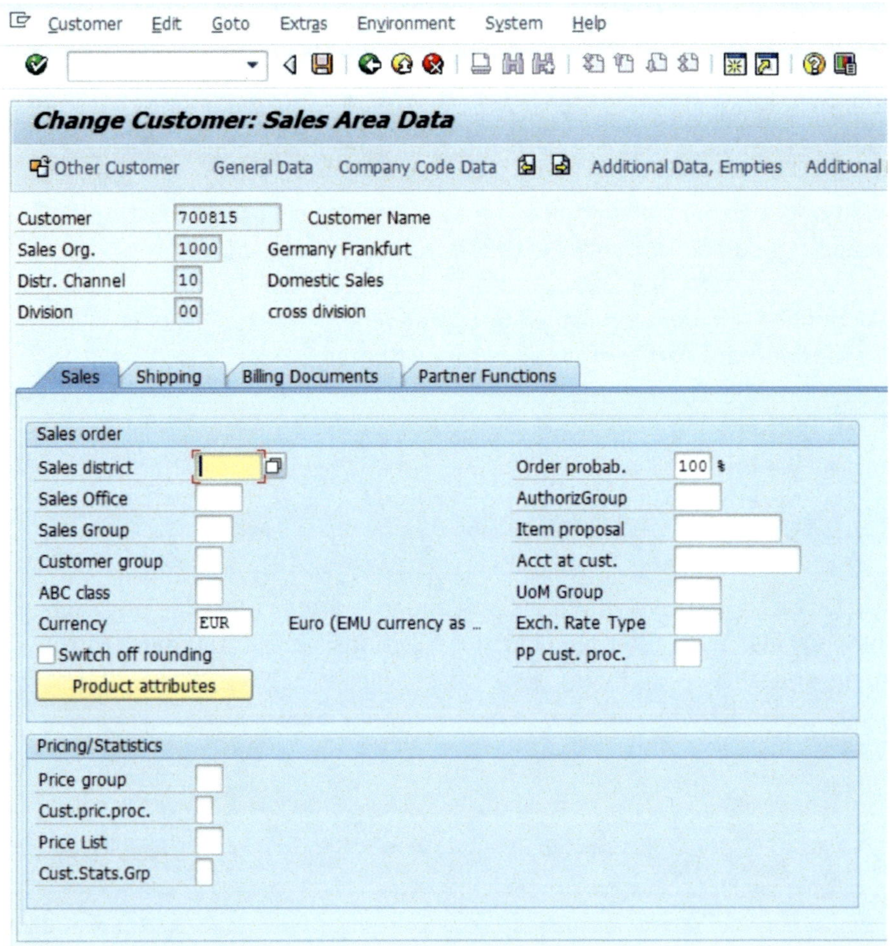

 Figure CM794

Customer Master Partner Functions:

A Customer is the entity that buy a service or a product. When we buy something from a shop we become a customer. Companies store customer information in their system for business functions. Customer information is essential for many different business transactions. For example, if customer want to ship his product to different location then we can call it alternative ship to, similarly bill to and payer also contains alternative partner functions. SAP Customer Master feature standard four partner functions, sold to, payer, bill to and ship to. Partner function defines additional detail of customer master. For example, one customers able to have many shipping partners, many payers and bill to partners.

Additional partner functions can be added to the customer master. Via creation of customer master with different account groups.

SAP defined a framework called best practices for customer master. There are four primary partner functions for customer master.

1. Sold to
2. Bill to
3. payer
4. Ship to

Above stated partner functions are standard partner function, but each company also uses additional partner functions for example sales rep, manager etc.

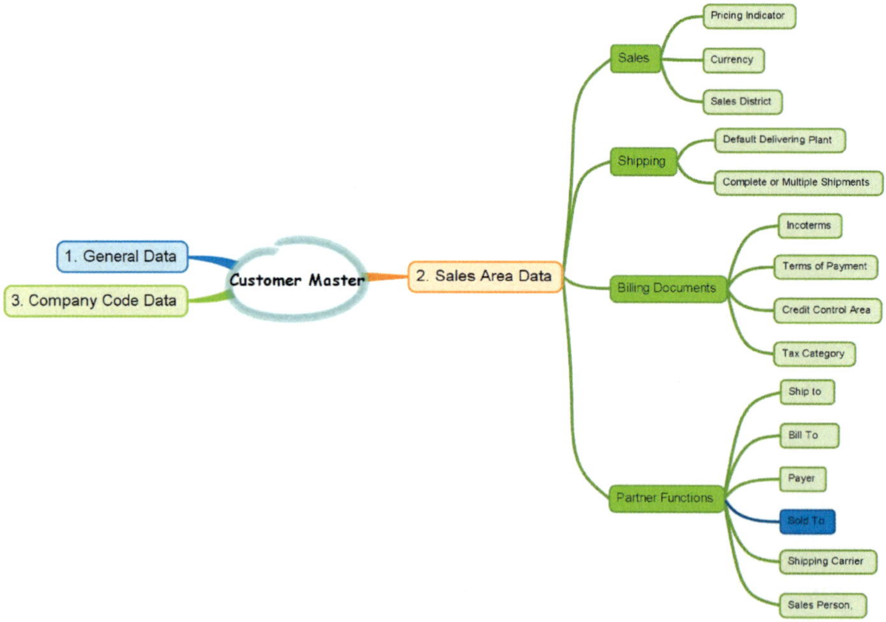

Figure CM795

Above figure C786 mind map display detail information after sales data view. Four additional four tabs represented after sales data view. Each view has many fields but in mind map only display most used fields, these fields might differ business to business. From sales tab pricing indicator controls the pricing procedure, currency defined for the customer currency and sales district used for reporting. Shipping tab contains delivering plant that get copied into sales order and complete and multiple shipment field controls if sales order needs to be completely shipped with one delivery or it can be shipped in multiple deliveries. From billing document tab: Payment term copied into sales order, credit control area defined for credit master. Tax category controls if customer taxable or tax exempt.

Sold to:

Sold to partner function represented as single unit record for a customer master partner function.

Bill to:

Each customer can have more than one bill to partner function for different billing information. SAP support multiple bill to partner function.

Ship to Partner function:

Each customer can have more than one ship to partner function for different shipping address. SAP support multiple bill to partner function.

Payer:

Each customer can have more than one bill to partner functions for the different payers. SAP support multiple bill to partner function.

Multiple Partner Information:

Figure CM796

Each customer master have multiple partner function expect from sold to.

Contact Person partner function:

Master data is utilized as a business partner's function in customer master. It able to create separately or entered while creating or changing customer.

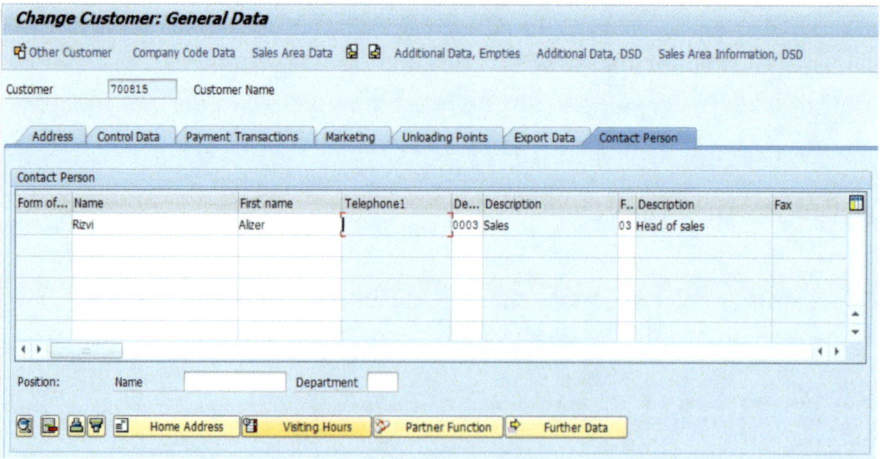

 Figure CM797

T-code for Contact person :

To Create VAP1
To Change VAP2
To Display VAP3

Additional Partner Functions:

The following is few examples of additional partner functions that can be configured and assigned to the customer master.

- Freight forwarder
- Sales representative
- Contact person

One Time Customer:

One-time customer is used when end customer information is not maintained in a system and we want to use it once for example customer that only buy the product at once.

Common Distribution Channel:

Common distribution channel is the customization in sales and distribution for defining common distribution channel for the master data. Based on this the sales org able to come under common distribution channel instead of extending sales that area to multiple distribution channel. This is also called referenced condition because the master data distribution channel is conditional record or grouping.

Common Division:

Common Division is utilized when grouping of division is required in the sales area into single common division. Common division streamlines the master data maintenance. While common sales can maintain from this function into common conditional master data for sales area use.

Customer Master T-codes:

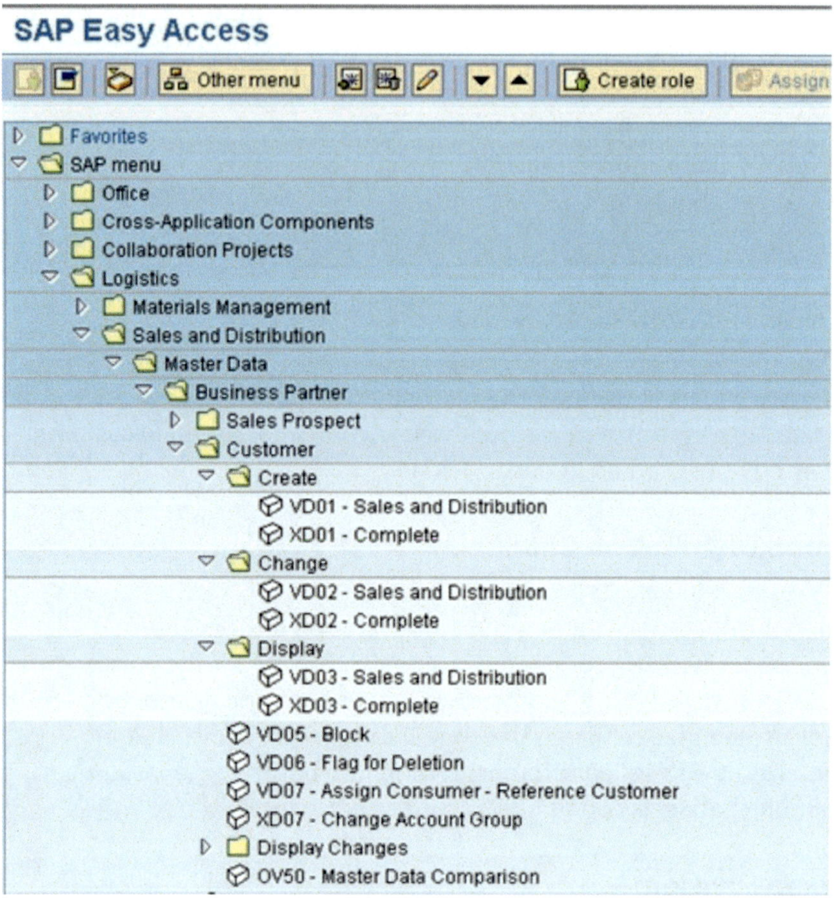

Figure CM798

NO	Description	T-code
1	Create Customer Master (Centrally)	**XD01**
2	Change Customer Master (Centrally)	**XD02**
3	Display Customer Master (Centrally)	**XD03**
4	Create Customer Master with Company Code View	FD01
5	Change Customer Master with Company Code View	FD02
6	Display Customer Master with Company Code View	FD03
7	Create Customer Master Sales View	VD01
8	Change Customer Master Sales View	VD02
9	Display Customer Master Sales View	VD03
10	**Block Customers**	**VD05**
11	**Delete Customer**	**VD06**
12	**Display Change's**	**VD04**
13	Mass update	XD99
14	Create Contact Person	VAP1

Mass updates allow multiple customers to change it at once. Display changes show When the customer master was changed and by which user.

Customer Master Tables:

The following some of the customer master tables:

Table	Description
KNA1	General Data
KNB1	Company Code Data
KNVV	Customer Sales Data
KNAT	Customer Master Tax Grouping
KNBK	Customer Master Back Detail
KNB5	Customer Master Dunning Data
KNKK	Customer Credit Management Data
KNMT	Customer Material Info Record Data
KNVI	Customer Master Tax Indicator
KNVP	Customer Master Partner Function

To view table, use T-code SE16N or SE16

How to Create Customer Master:

Creating a customer master centrally (XD01) means all required views of customers are maintained with full access. Creating a customer master with finance view (FD01) means two views are maintained, such as General Data and Company code data. Creating a customer master (VD01) with sales view means two view of customer master is maintained hence sales view and general data.

Transaction Code: XD01

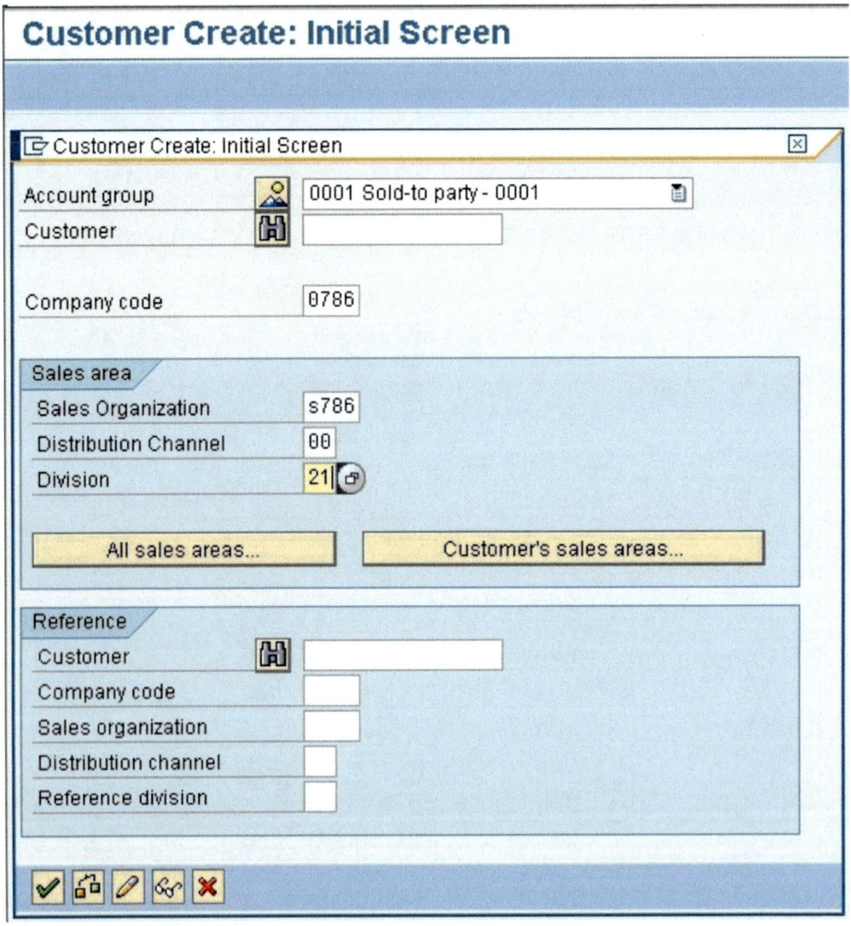

Figure CM799

To create customer master select account group, enter company code and sales area information.

Based on account group either number will be selected or it may require the user to enter customer number, every company define controls for customer master selection for customer number. In most cases customer number selection automatic and next available determine by system.

To create customer users needs to enter all required field and save the customer. If requires field are no entered in system it will not save the customer and display warning massage to enter required fields.

Tips:
To make customer creation process fast it would be beneficial to use reference customer number. By using reference customer, all of the reference customer fields will be copied over to new customer expect from general data.

General Data View:

Address Tab:

Fields with check box indicating those fields are required fields, fields without check box in them are optional fields.

Enter customer name, address and required data in general data view of address tab of customer master. First screenshot in figure CR787, display empty field and in figure CR788 all required entries are maintained.

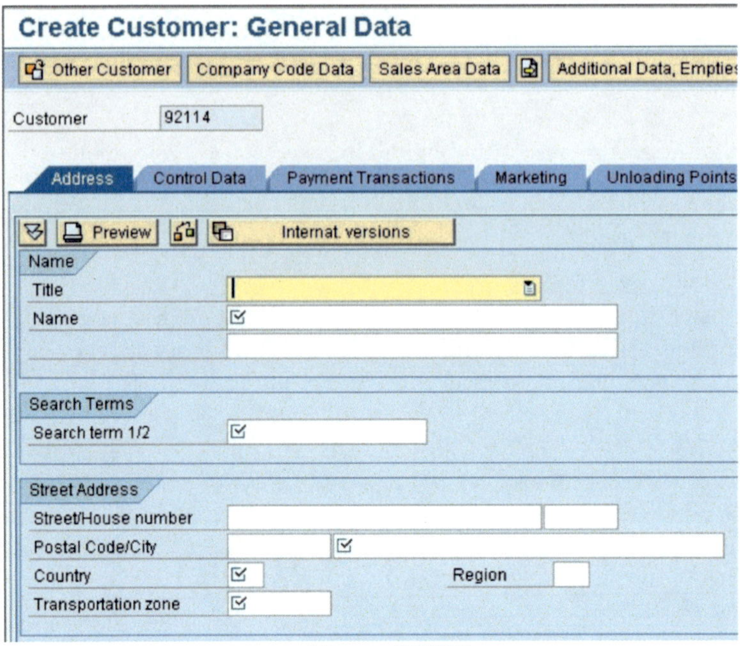

Figure CR787

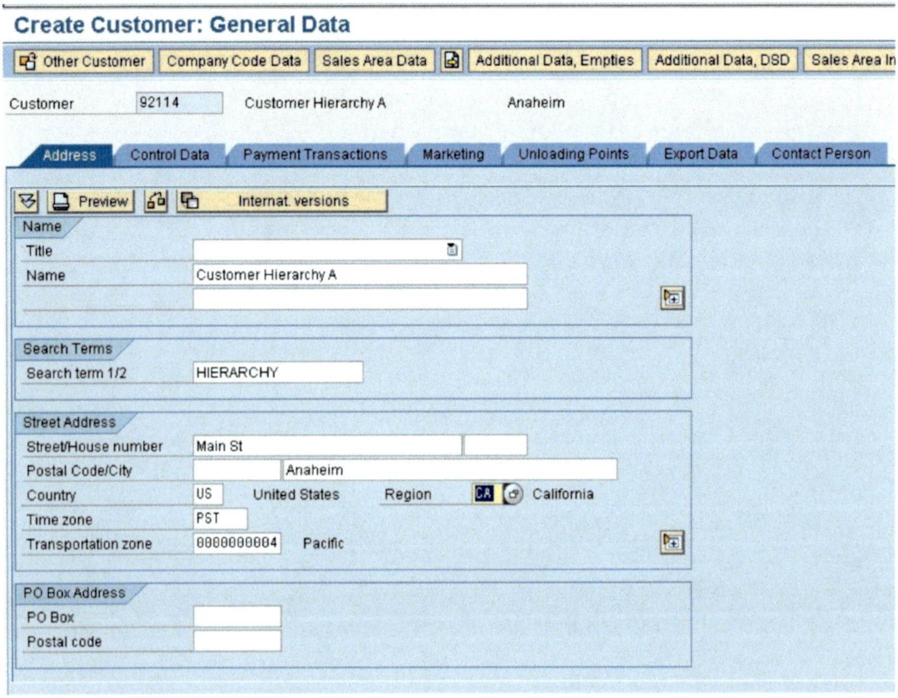

Figure CR788

Control Data Tab:

Vendor and industry important field figure CR789.

Vendor: Vendor number maintains in this field if customer also setup as a vendor too. A Vendor created in SAP from VK01.

Industry: Industry key field categories define different types of industry indicator. Industry key also helpful for report to segregate customer groups. Additional fields also available in customer classification and additional data but this field used with many different combinations.

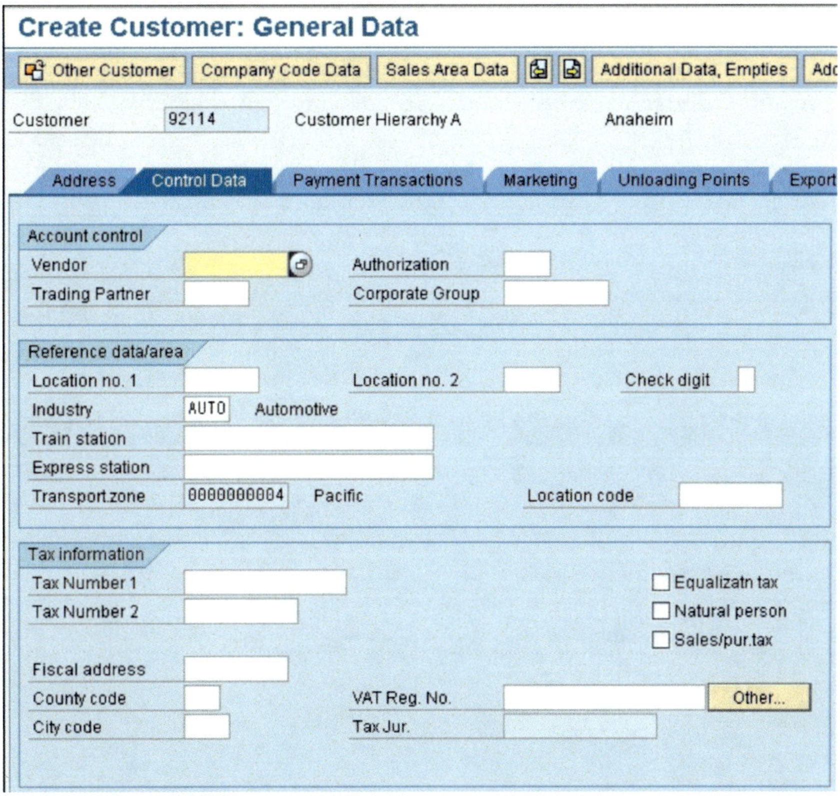

Figure CR789

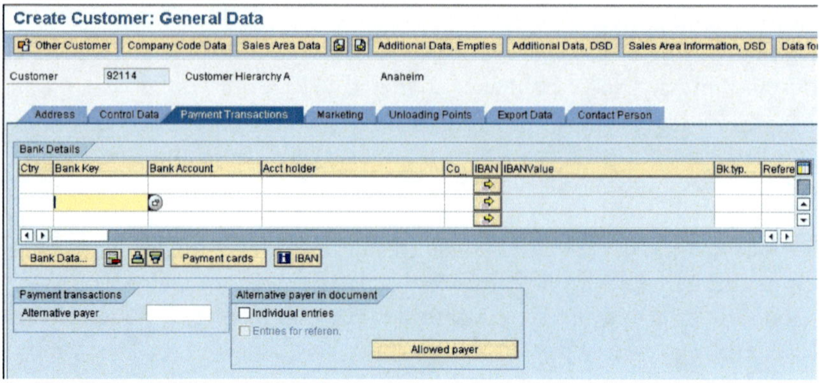

Figure CR790

Payment transaction:

In this tab user payment information stored with the bank and ACH information. Reference for payment transaction in figure CR790.

Note: The interesting point to be noted that when customer is created two additional tab appease "export data" and "contact person."

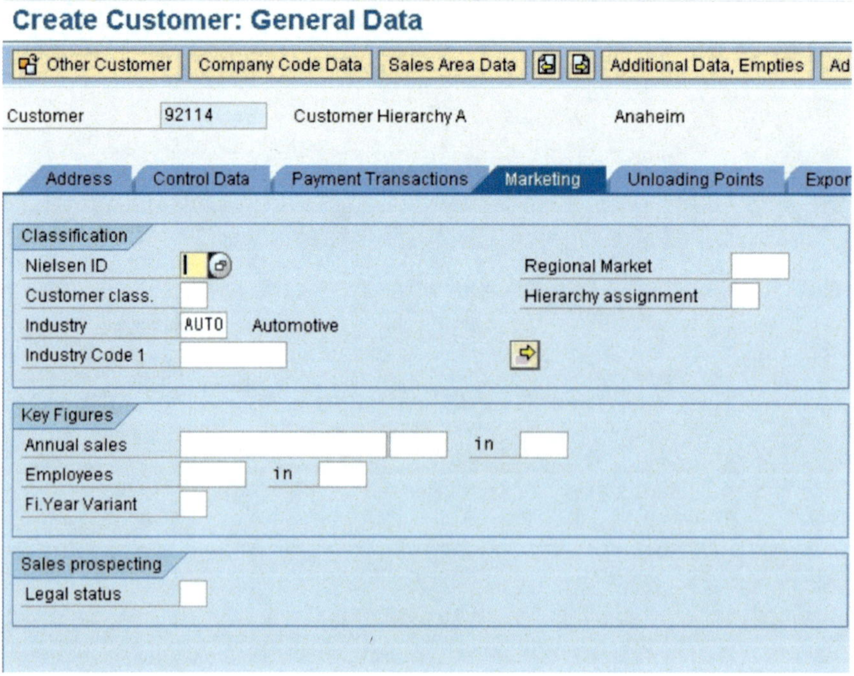

Figure CR791

Marketing Tab:

In figure CR91 review marketing tab view with marketing relevant fields. In customer master not, all the fields are used but many field provided by SAP for companies to use them if needed.

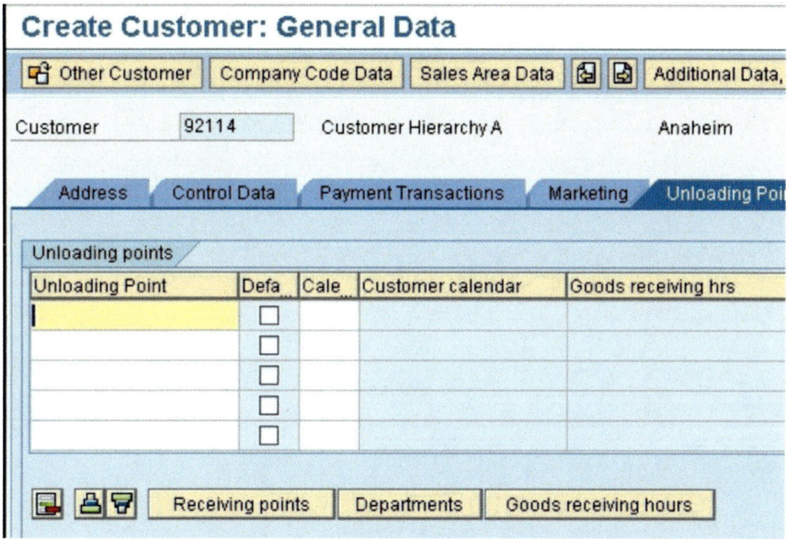

Figure CR792

Unloading Point Tab:

Unloading tab used to define customer good receiving delivery points, good receiving timings. Good receiving points added for a customer for example department store, door, hall, shop floor, etc. If good receiving hours are not defined system will create delivery any time.

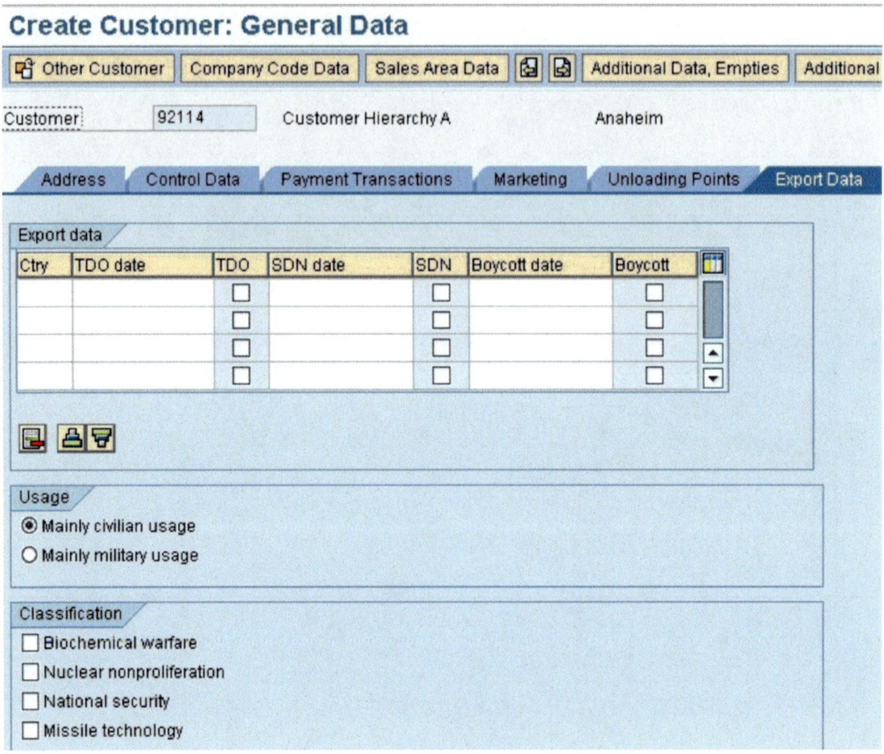

Figure CR793

Export Data:

Export data reference from figure CR793. Export data tab is very less frequently used area. In this section customers are maintained for import export related process. In this view customer can be marked if they are relevant for civilian or military with further classification.

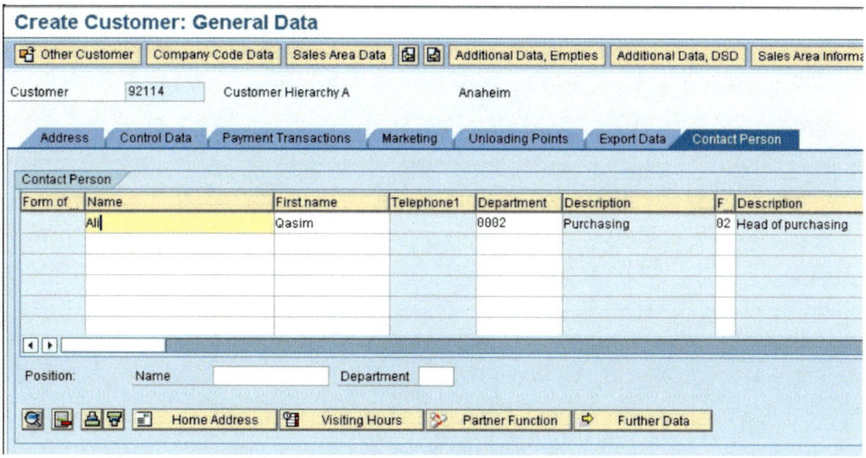

Figure CR794

Contact person:

Reference from figure CR794, in this customer tab we enter customer contact persons. Many different contact persons entered with their detail information including phone number and email.

Additional contact person can be added from customer creation or by following t-codes.

T-code for Contact person:

To Create VAP1
To Change VAP2
To Display VAP3

Each contact person also contain additional information reference figure CR795 display detailed view of contact information.

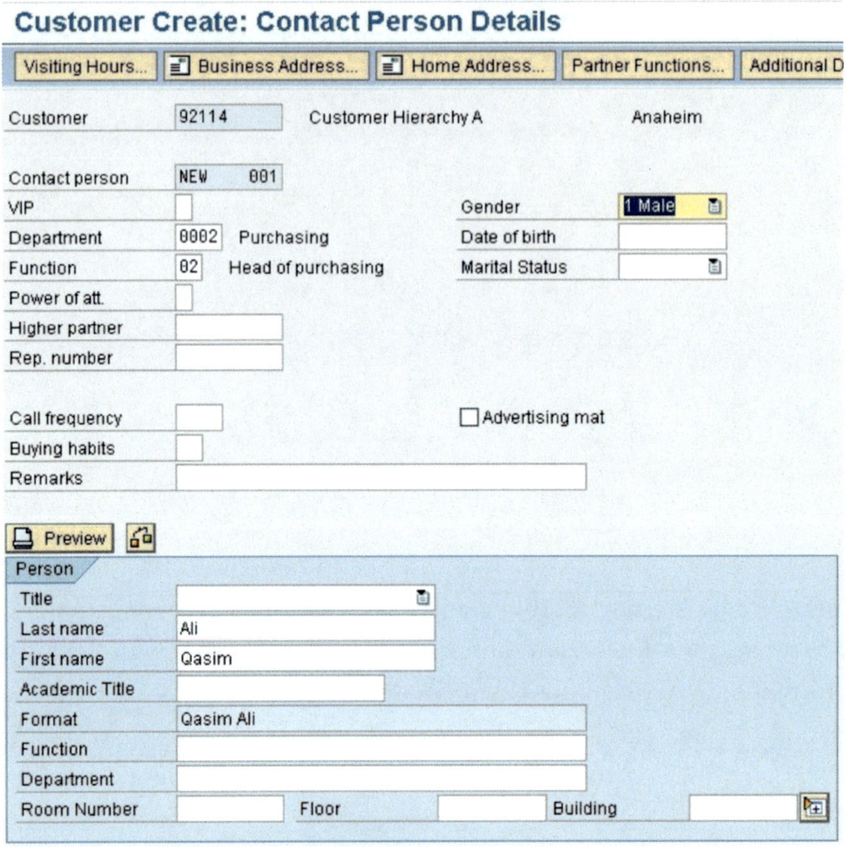

Figure CR795

Sales Area View:

How to go into customer sales area? click on sales area of customer master. In sales area data it display on top "sales area data."

Sales data view contains fields which are relevant for sales order, shipment delivery and invoice process. Detailed information defined in each tab relevant topics.

Sales Area View: Sales

In sales tab sales order related fields are used. Currency for sales order is defined in this view, Item proposal contain most used item proposal number which can default set of frequently ordered materials. Pricing relevant fields used for pricing determination in sales order. Customer hierarchy used for setup of customer hierarchy.

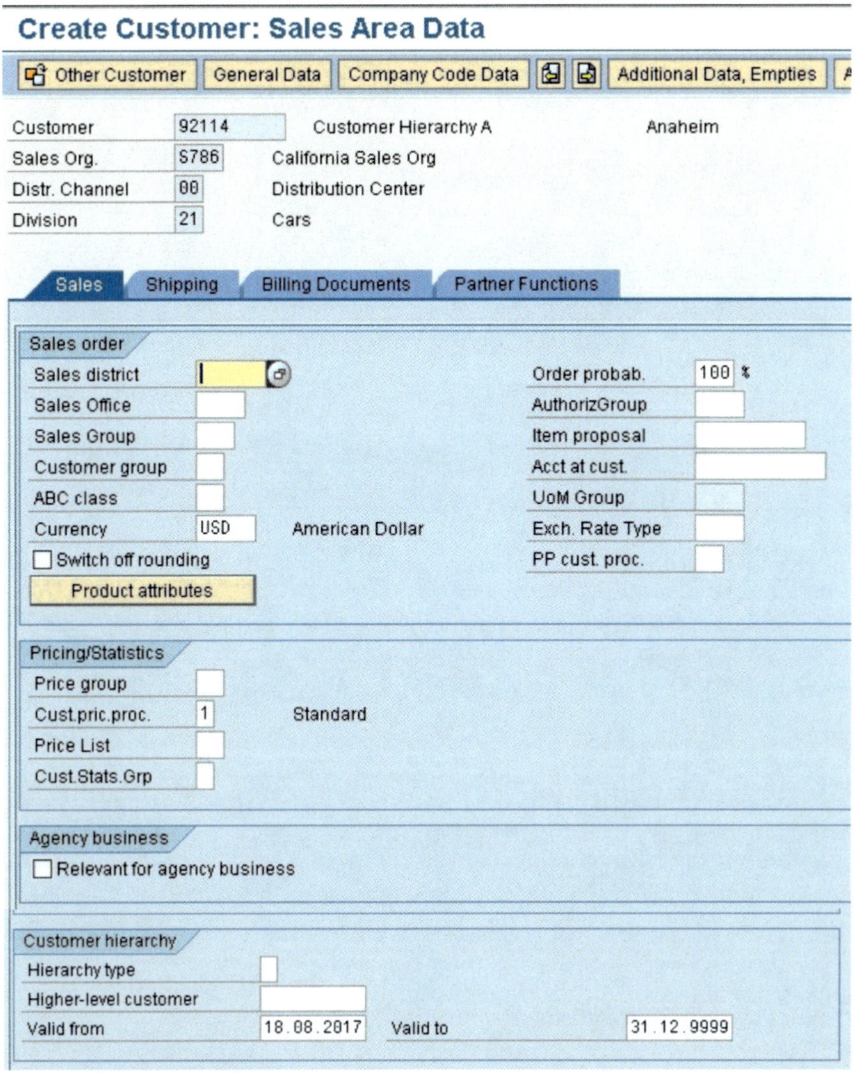

Figure CR796

Sales Area View: Shipping:

Shipping condition used for storage location determination in sales order. **Delivery priority** set in the system to priorities deliveries. Delivery priority used for allocation process to allocate orders. **Partial delivery per Item** field control if this customer should receive complete delivery or a single delivery. From screenshot figure CR797 option is selected to allow partial delivery.

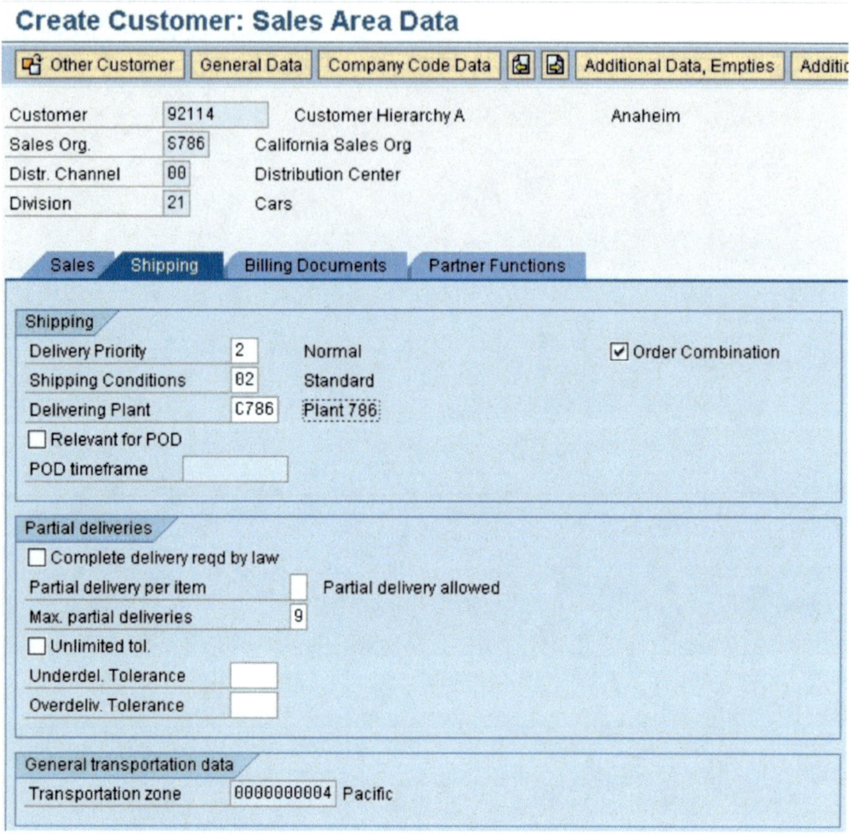

Figure CR797

Sales Area View: Billing Document

In screenshot reference CR798 billing document tab display billing relevant fields. **Terms of payment** field value copy from customer master to sales order. Invoice date controls billing date for a customer. Tax classification defines if a customer should be libel to tax or tax exempt for reference screenshot Figure CR798 and CR800.

Credit Control area used for credit master for a customer, chapter number 4 cover this topic in detail.

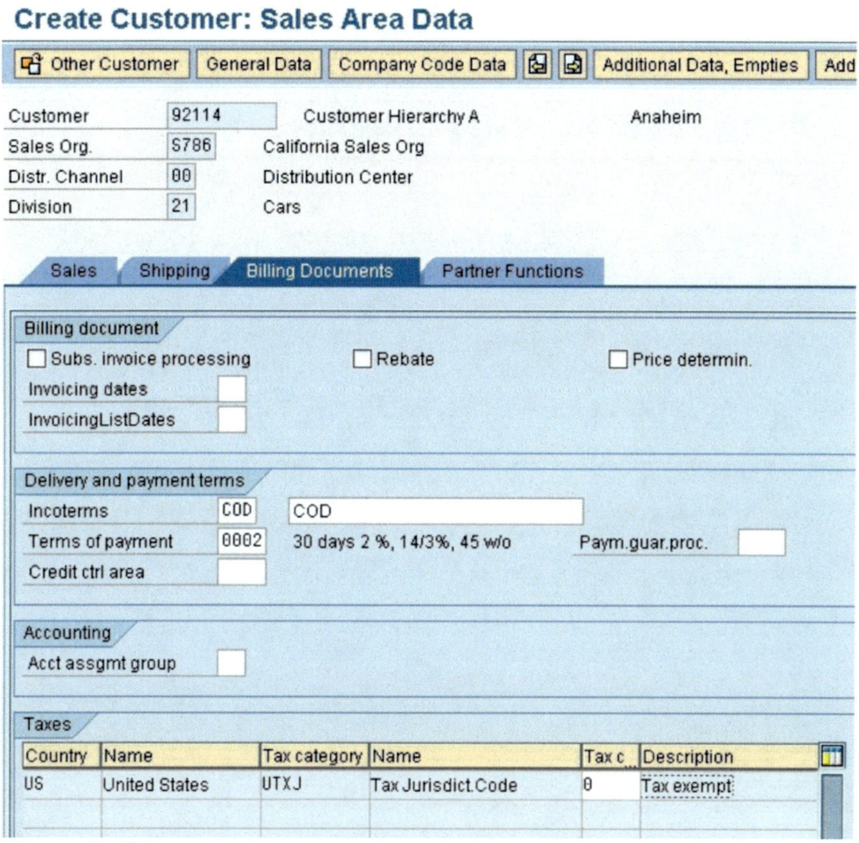

Figure CR798

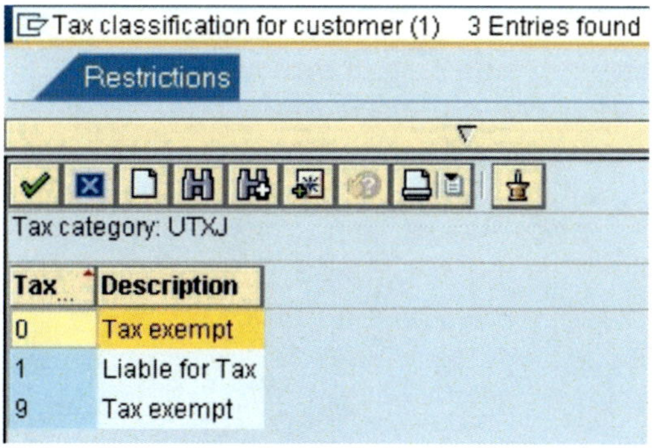

Figure CR800

Sales Area View: Partner Function

Customer partner function is entered in this view.
alternative, ship to, bill to and payer entered in partner function view

screenshot CR801. Additional alternative partners are created with their account group and then these partner function added in this view.

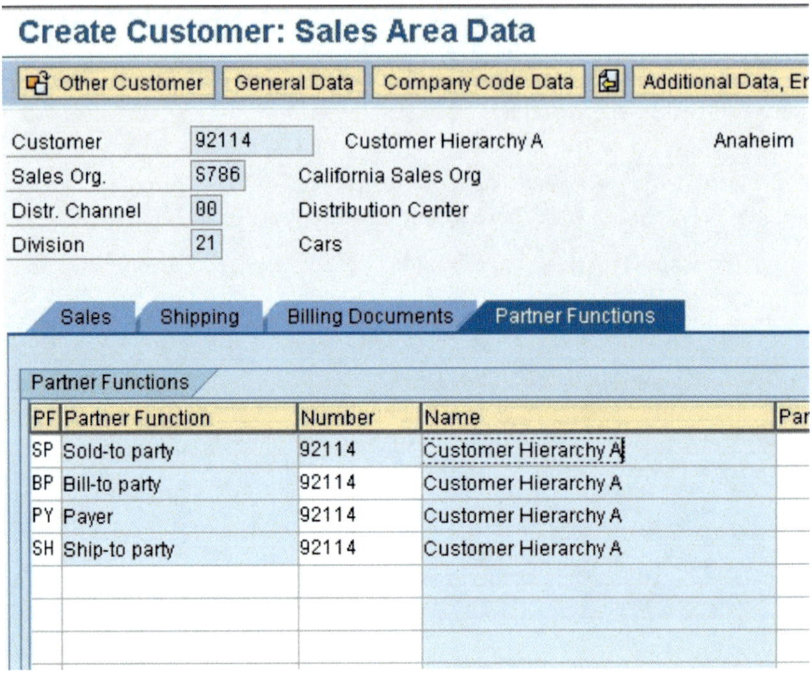

Figure CR801

Company Code View

Company Code View: Account Management tab screenshot reference CR8002. Recon account field represents reconciliation account for a customer master. Recon account record general leader account for customer receivables.

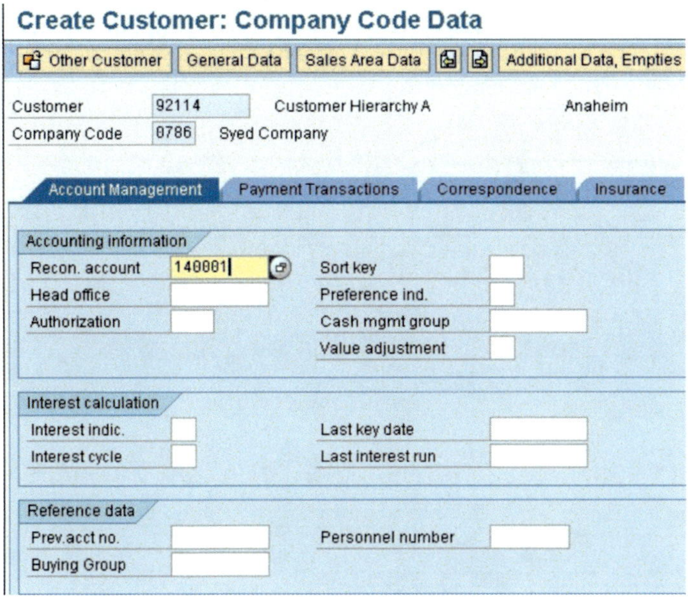

Figure CR802

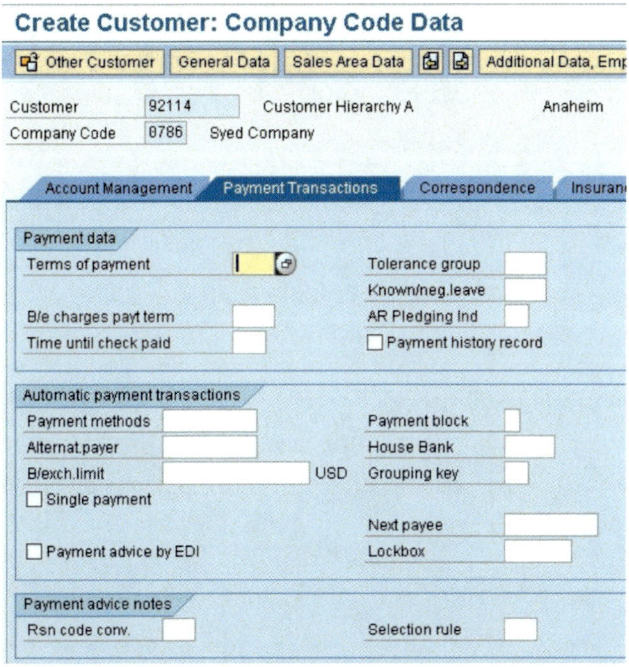

Figure CR803

Figure CR803 payment transaction tab contains payment data, automatic transactions methods.

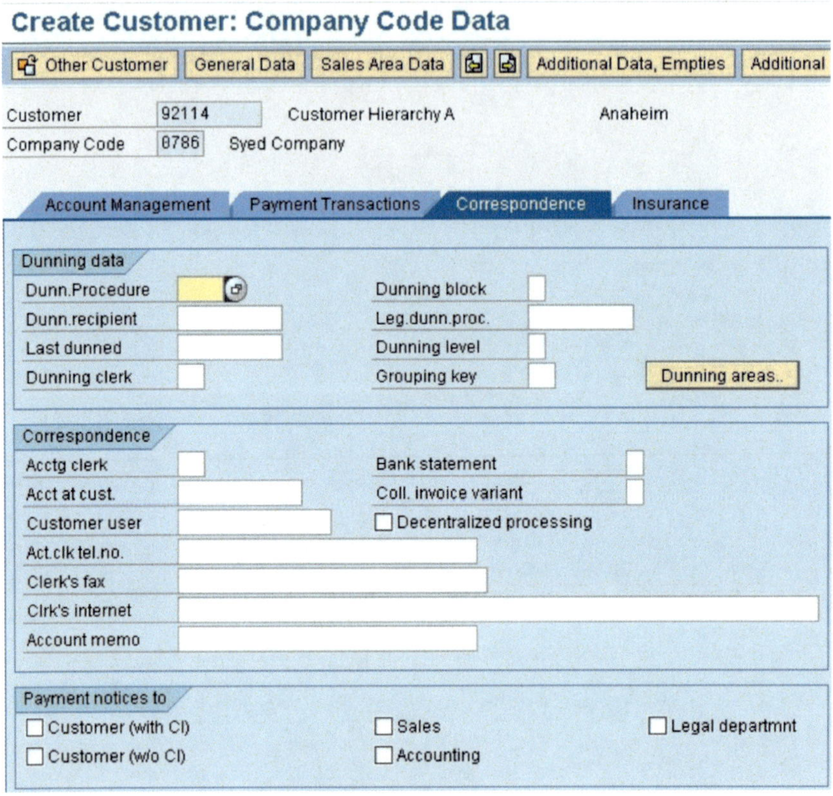

Figure CR804

Figure CR804 display sceenshot of company code data: Correspondence view. In this view dunning procedures are controls used for dunning. Also correspondence and payment notice also more options available for customer master.

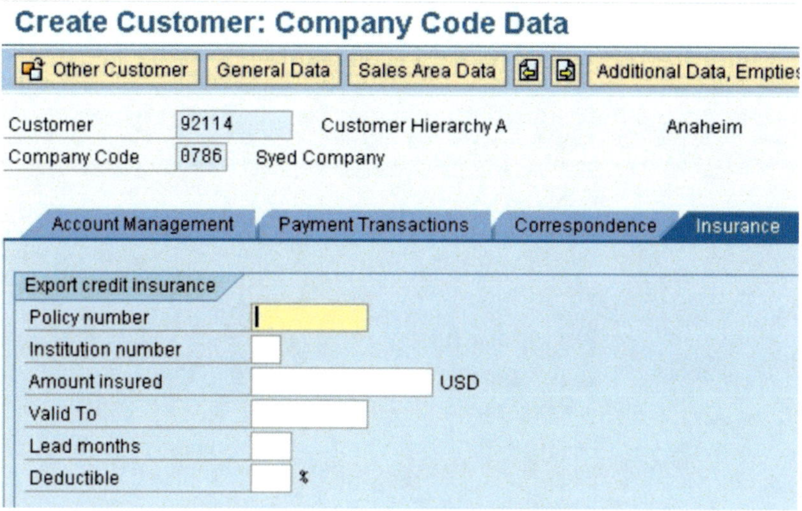

Figure CR805

Figure CR804 display scheenshot of company code data: insurance view.

Additional Information

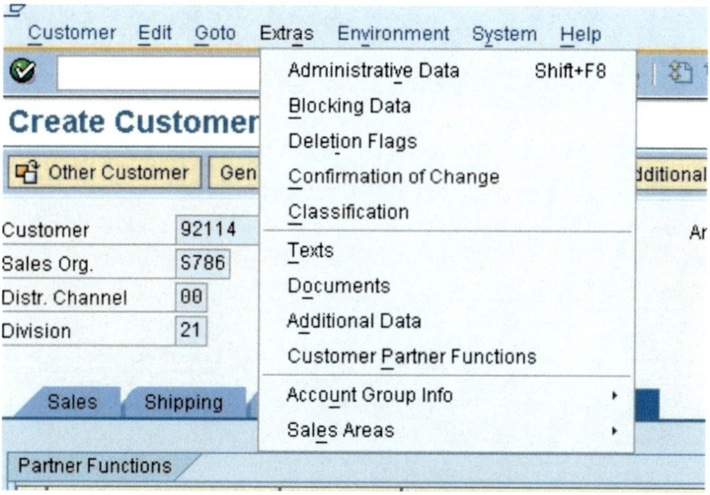

Figure CR806

From each view of a customer are there are different sets of fields available for customer master. In screenshot CR805 these sets of fields are available for users to maintain these fields. If customer setup in multiple sales areas it can be reviewed from the screenshot CR807 by selecting sales areas by customer. In additional data used for additional customer groups screenshot CR808. Additional customer data also available from general data view screenshot reference CR809.

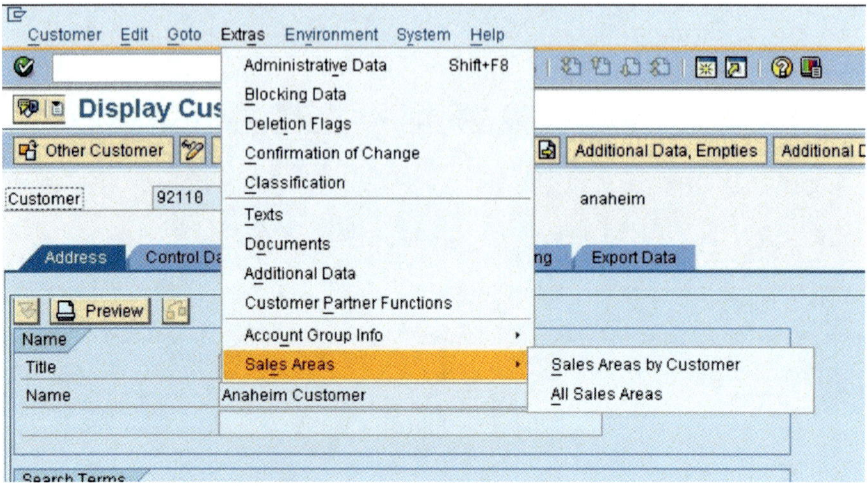

Figure CR807

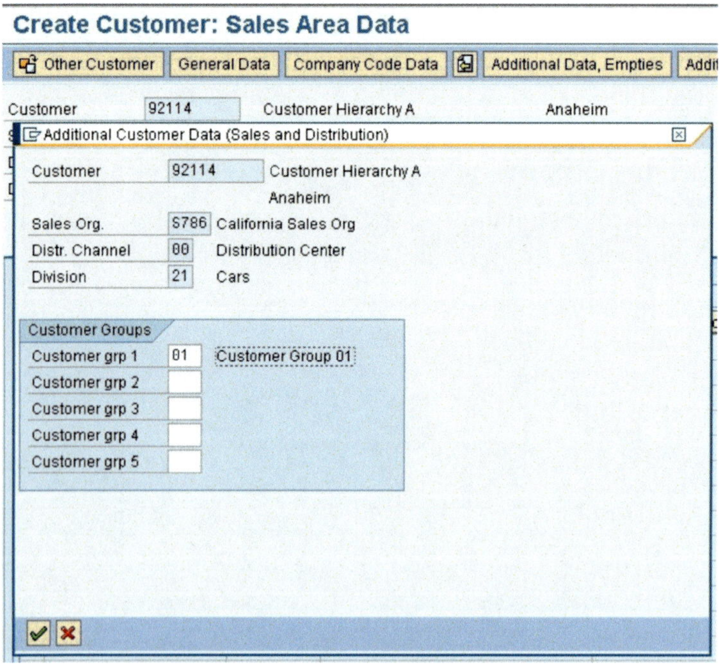

Figure CR808

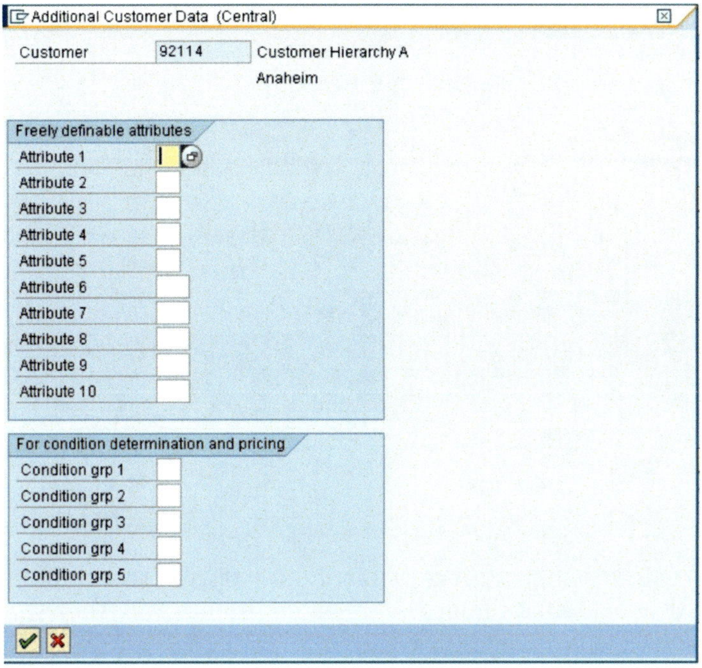

Figure CR809

Customer additional information can be accessed by clicking "Extra" screenshot CR806.

- Blocking Data
- Deletion Flags
- Confirmation of Change
- Classification
- Texts
- Documents
- Additional Date

Customer Reports:

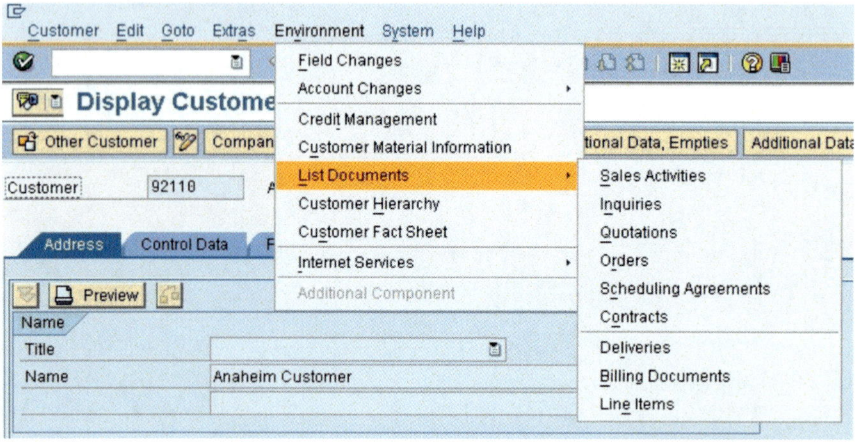

Figure CR810

Relevent customer reports per transaction will display screenshot CR810.

- Inquiries
- Quotation
- Order
- Schdule agreements
- Contacts
- Delivries
- Billing Docuemnts
- Line Items

Blocka and Unblock Customer

To block or unblock customer use transaction code: VD05

Enter Customer number and sales area to process to block or unblock screenshot reference CR811.

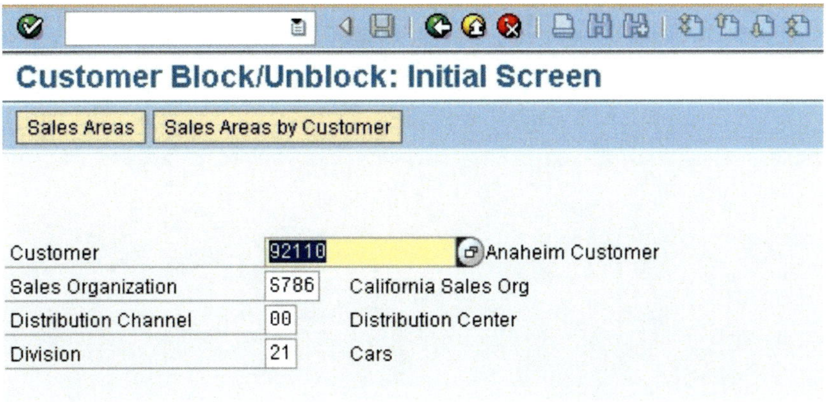

Figure CR811

Customer can be blocked for single or multiple sales areas.

Customer Deletion:

A customer can be marked for deletion.
T-code: VD06

Enter a customer number and sales area. Customers can be marked for deletion for all sales area or single sales area. Deletion flag also can be marked on general data.

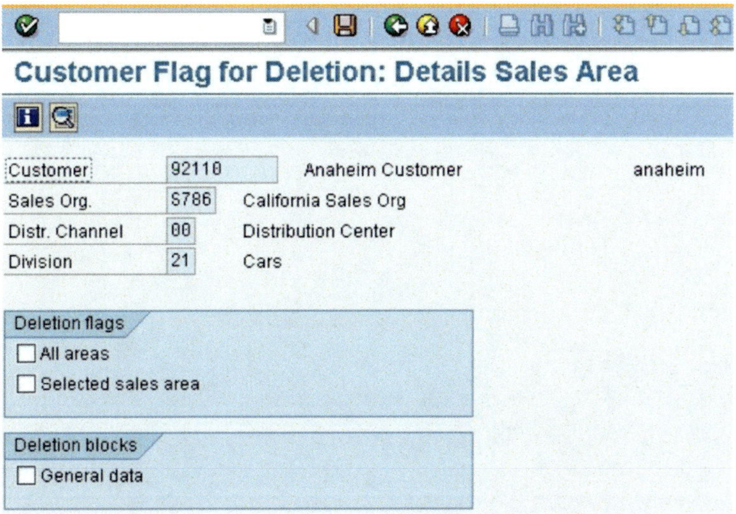

Figure CR812

Notes:

Chapter 4

Customer Credit Management

Customer Credit Management
Credit Limit
Credit Control area

Credit Control Area:

Credit Control area used independently or centrally managed. Credit control area controls the customer's credit functionality. The credit control area should have the same currency as company's code. Each company's code with one credit control assigned to it, but credit control able to have many company codes assigned to it. The credit control area also able to assign to multiple company codes. The credit control area is utilized in customer credit master creation.

Credit Management:

Credit management is the combination of risk category and credit control area of credit master. Customer credit is created after customer creation. The credit limit automatically blocks transactions when the credit limit is reached. Credit functionality able to utilize to block sales order, delivery, and billing documents. Customer credit is calculated against the customer's open document and credit exposure.

What is Customer Credit Exposure?

Credit exposure is combination of open orders, open deliveries and open invoices. Credit exposure is considered a customer's open sales orders, liabilities, delivery, billing, and posting open document's value, which then adds them all together. The credit exposure is utilized for credit controls for the transactions to be blocked.

Customer Credit Exposure = Open Order + Open Deliveries + Open Invoices

Types of credit check:

There are two types of credit check available for customers.

1. Simple Credit check
2. Automatic Credit check (Static and Dynamics)

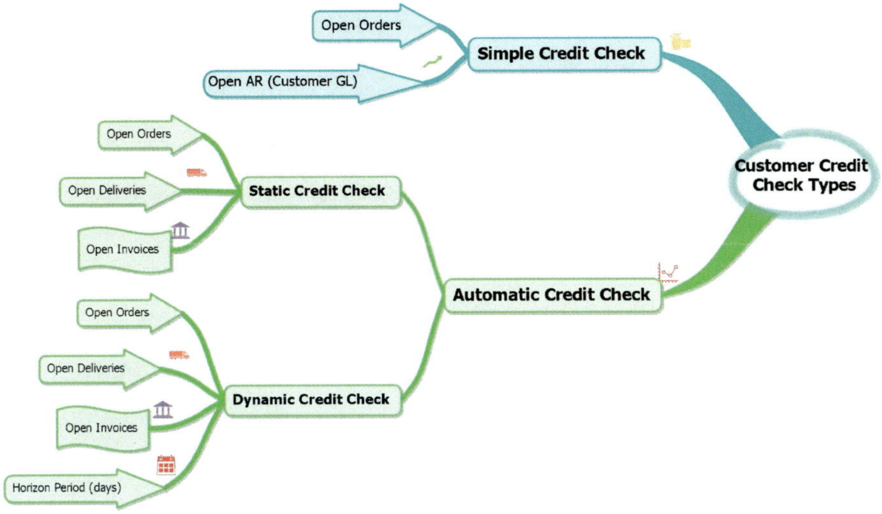

Figure CR814

Mind map from figure CR814 display different types of credit check available, simple and automatic credit check. All different types of credit check differs with company to company. it is important to understand what credit check implemented in the company. Base on different credit check each company adopt different procedures and trainings, this book covers SAP standard credit checks for users.

Simple Credit Check:

Simple credit check only considers open AR item against new order. if open AR is higher than credit limit then new order will be on credit block.

Automatic credit check:

Automatic credit check has two types of credit check but both credit check consider credit exposure. Credit exposure means open order plus open deliveries and open invoices.

Static Credit Check:

Static credit check calculates open orders + open deliveries + open invoices and if combination of these documents increases the credit limit, new order will be on credit block.

Dynamic Credit check:

Dynamic credit check calculates open orders + open deliveries + open invoices if combination of these documents increases the credit limit new order will be on credit block.

Credit Master (FD32)

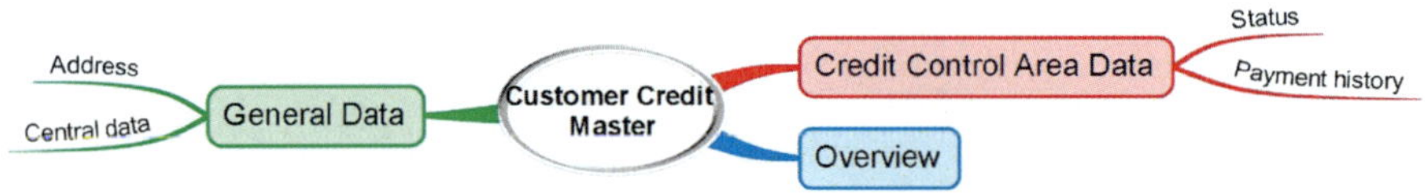

Figure CR815

Credit master is created with the combination of customer and credit control area. Credit is based on credit limit and credit risk assigned to the customer. Credit is calculated based on the horizon and credit exposure. Credit exposure means it's an open order, open delivery and open invoice. In credit control area risk category is assigned to determine credit block.

T-code for credit management is FD32
T-code to display Credit Master FD33

The following are 5 different views of credit master:

- Overview
- Address
- Central data

- Status
- Payment history

Overview:

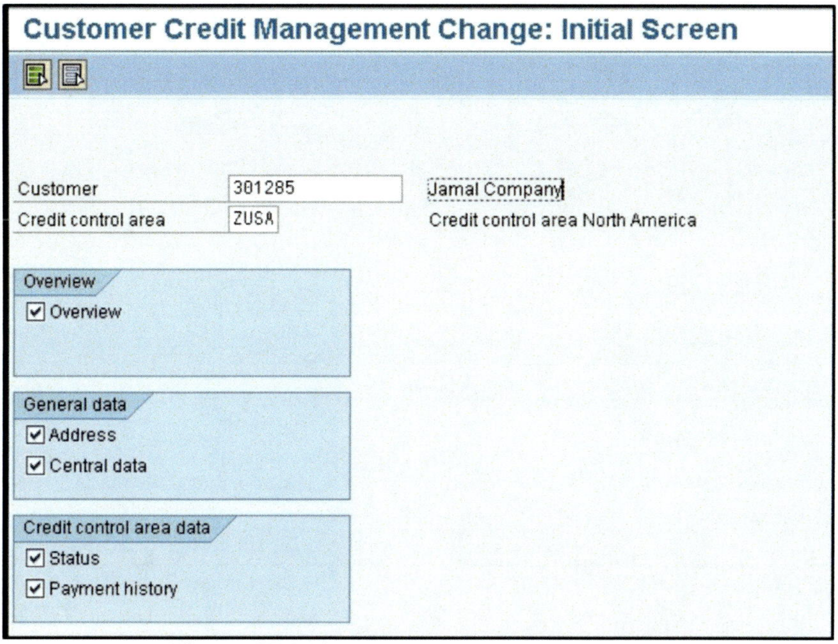

Figure CR816

To view customer credit master, enter t-code FD32, in screenshot CR16 enter customer number and enter credit control area and select a view that need to be reviewed. As per selection relevant views will be displayed in customer credit management.

Overview:

First tab or view from customer credit management called "overview" figure CR817. In overview customer total credit limit, exposure and credit limit used display based on open documents. From customer account revisable payment history display with cash discount and without cash discount. In dunning data, dunning related values are maintained. In control risk category is assigned for credit management and credit group assigned for the users who are reasonable for reporting and credit release transactions. From controls a customer can be marked blocked.

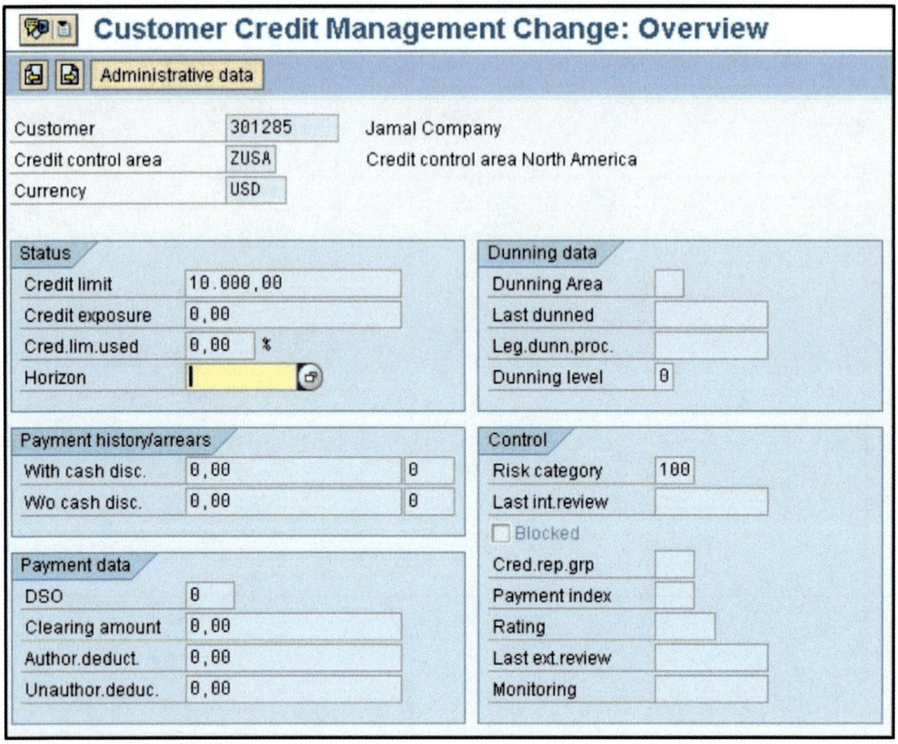

Figure CR817

General Data: Address

Address data view screenshot in figure CR818, where user review customer address data. Address data view is very self-explanatory.

General Data: Central Data

Central data view screenshot in figure CR819. Total amount and largest individual limit ““10,000” represent credit control area limit for “ZUSA” where maximum permitted credit limit defined as “100,000”.

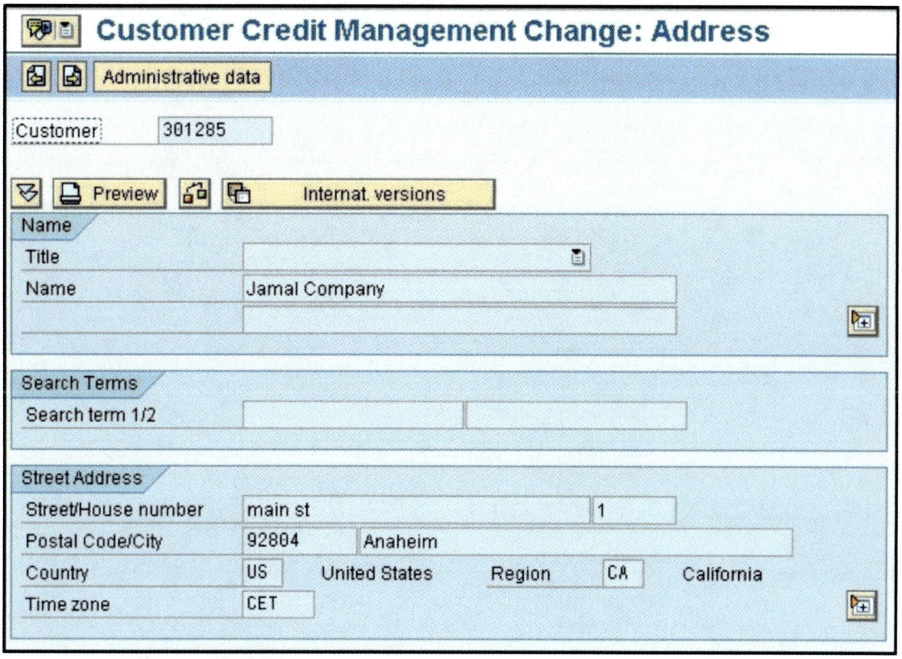

Figure CR818

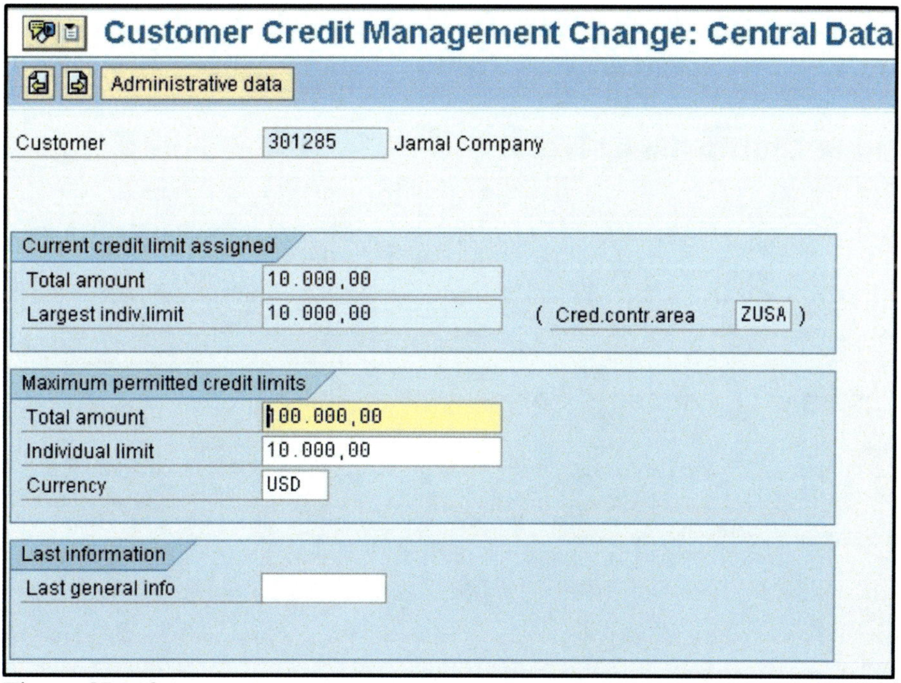

Figure CR819

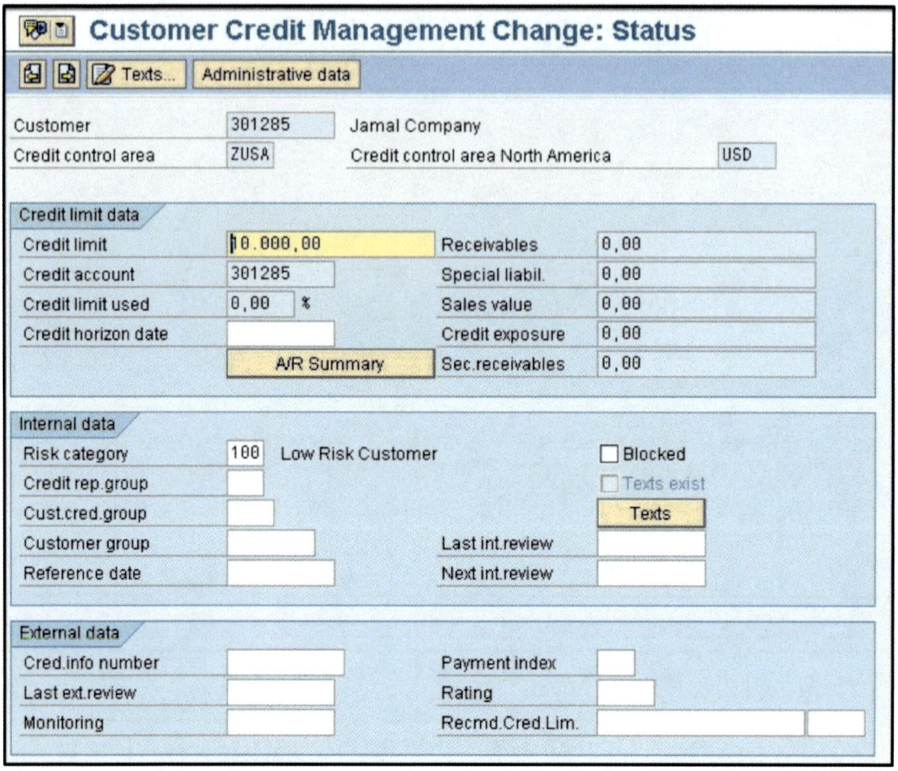

Figure CR820

Credit Control Data: Status

A customer could be assigned to multiple credit control areas and status view help user to view credit area limit in this view. In this view we can review selected "customer selected credit control area" credit limit. In figure CR820 credit control area display on top under the customer number.

Customer: Payment History

Customer (AR) account receivable postings status is relevant to posted or open. In this view of payment history from figure CR821 user review payment history of customer master.

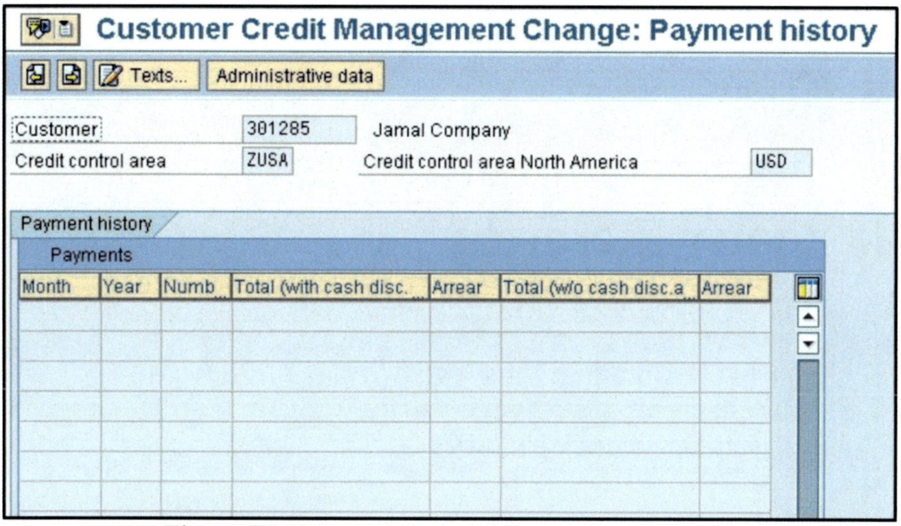

Figure CR821

Customer credit block:

Customer credit block controls and stops the sales and delivery of a document for further processing. The sales order requires processing of approval to release it from the credit block. The credit block able to remove with the work list report and by following T-codes:

- VKM4 Release credit for sales order and Delivery document
- VKM3 Release credit for sales document
- VKM5 Release credit for Delivery Document

Chapter 5

Customer Hierarchy

- **Customer Hierarchy Introduction**
- **How to create Customer Hierarchy**
- **Display Customer Hierarchy**

Customer Hierarchy:

Customer hierarchy used for business process for pricing and rebates. SAP Customer hierarchy defined with customers assigned at different levels. Hierarchy primarily useful for pricing, rebates, partner functions, etc. Customer hierarchy based on SAP partner types and sales area assignment.

Customer hierarchy simplification in mind map:

Figure H786

Figure H786 display different fields from customer hierarchy. Customer hierarchy has validly period with start and end dates. Customer hierarchy contain address information, it contains sales area data, it contains indicator for rebate, it contains pricing indicator and how higher-level customer in hierarchy assignment. Please review customer hierarchy with a screenshot of figure H787. Sales area data display in customer assignment from lover level customer to higher level customer. Relevant for pricing indicate if the customer hierarchy relevant for pricing.

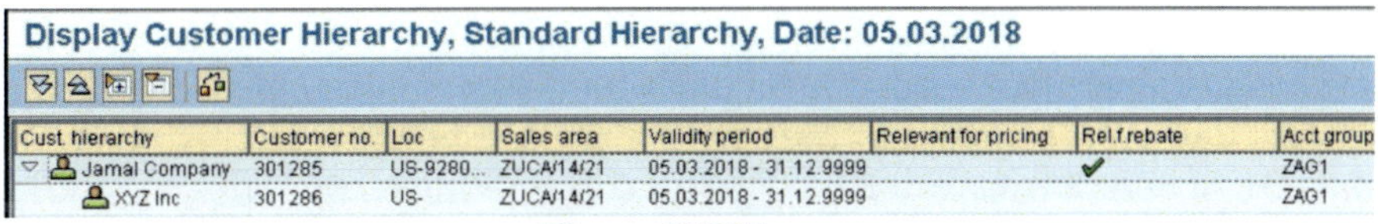
Display Customer Hierarchy, Standard Hierarchy, Date: 05.03.2018

Cust. hierarchy	Customer no.	Loc	Sales area	Validity period	Relevant for pricing	Rel.f.rebate	Acct group
Jamal Company	301285	US-9280...	ZUCA/14/21	05.03.2018 - 31.12.9999		✔	ZAG1
XYZ Inc	301286	US-	ZUCA/14/21	05.03.2018 - 31.12.9999			ZAG1

Figure H787

Customer Hierarchy for Rebate:

Customer hierarchy used for a customer where we would pay to the higher level customer rebate if lower level customers but products. In this scenarios contract can be written for company or group and calculation will be calculated based on sub branches buying products.

How to Create Customer hierarchy:

Customer hierarchy transaction code: **VDH1N**

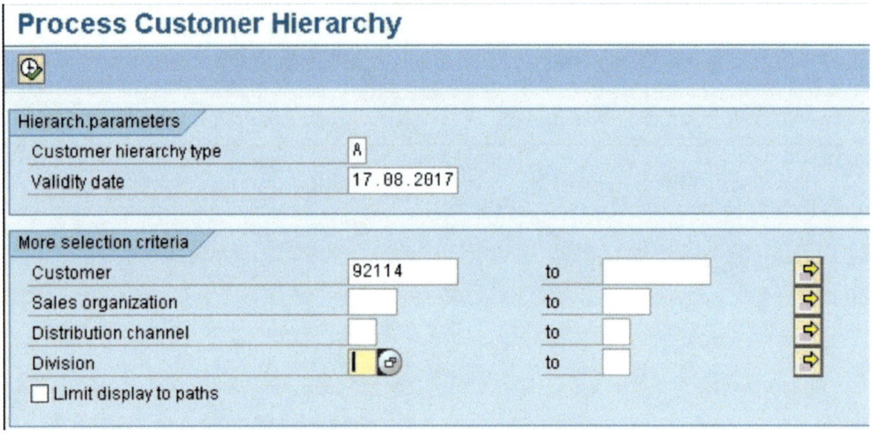

Figure H787

Customer hierarchy type:

In this field use SAP standard hierarchy type: "A." Many companies use custom hierarchy type so, please use as per company defined hierarchy type.

Validity Date:

Use this field to enter the validity date for customer hierarchy. After initial screen validity also maintain on every level of customer hierarchy.

Customer Number:

Enter the customer number that is required for customer hierarchy. All additional lower level customers are added in 2nd screen figure H788 display detail view of additional customers used on customer hierarchy.

Sales Organization:

Enter sales organization used for customer hierarchy.

Distribution Channel:

Enter the distribution number.

Division:

Enter the division number.

For customer hierarchy creation required fields are following:

- Customer hierarchy type
- Validity date
- Customer Number

Optional data "sales area data" is entered in 2nd detailed screen with customer hierarchy assignment.

From figure H787 click on execute button or "F8" to execute.

2nd Screen:

New Screen will come up as reference screenshot figure "H788". All of steps to assignment from higher level to lower level maintained in this screen.

From figure "H788" On the left screen with arrow click on blank page icon, to start customer assignments.

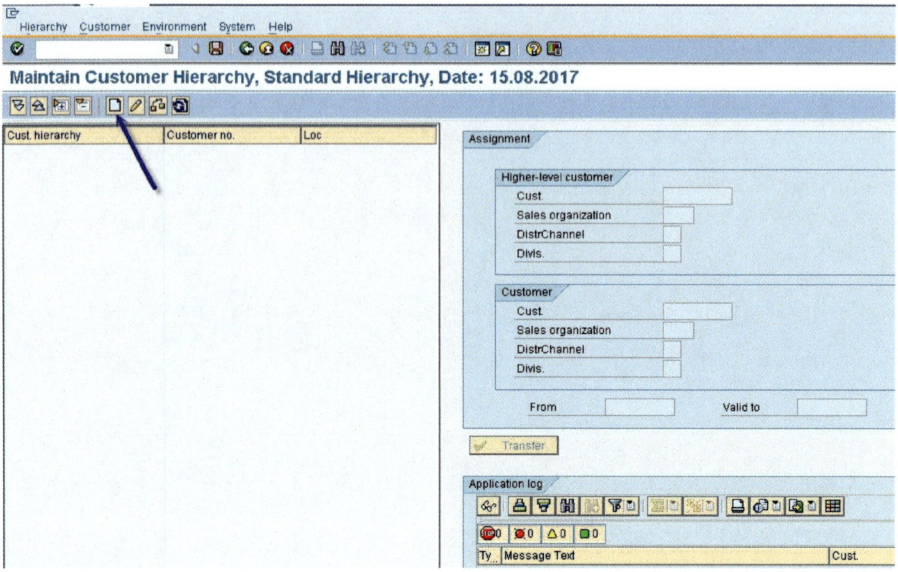

Figure H788

By clicking new button, assignment area will be available for entries for higher level customer to lover level customer.

In figure H789 customer to assigned to higher-level customer with validity date. Customer number required with sales area and higher-level customer also required with customer number with higher-level sales area.

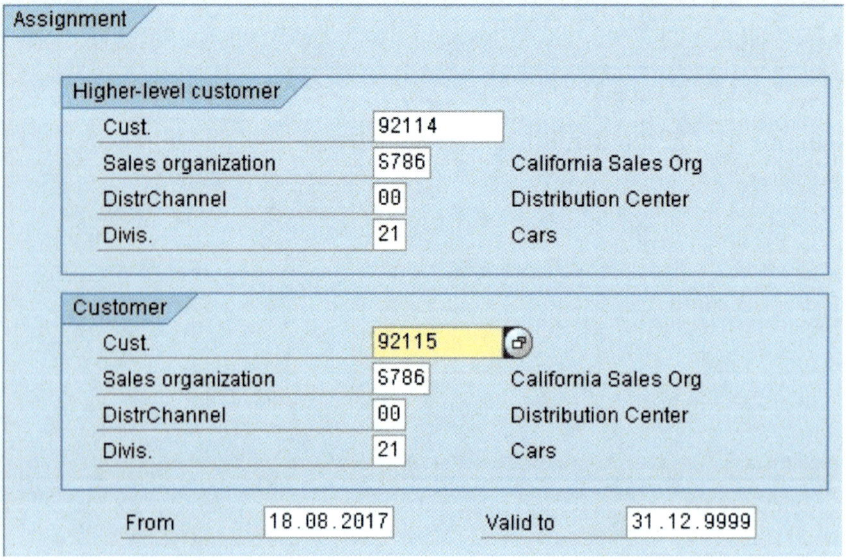

Figure H789

After entering all the field, press enter, and system will display massage and display customer assignment, if the entries are valid. If there is issue with customer assignment error will display in application log. If there is error red icon along with error massage will display and for success massage green icon will display.

With successful assignment, customer child and parent relation will display in left side of the screen. Customer assignments increase as more child and parent relationship created. Left side of higher level customer triangle activated to display and hide lower level customer reference screenshot figure H790.

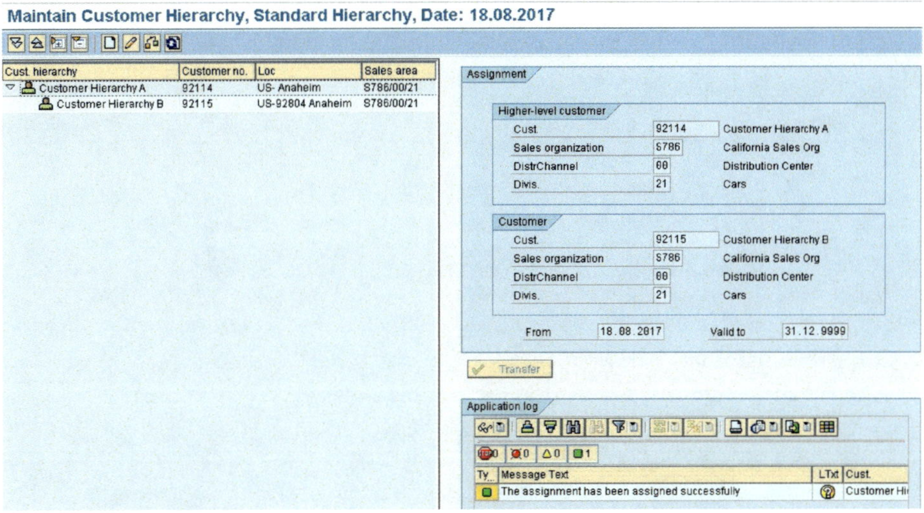

Figure H790

If we click on triangle icon in left we can review customer hierarchy tree.

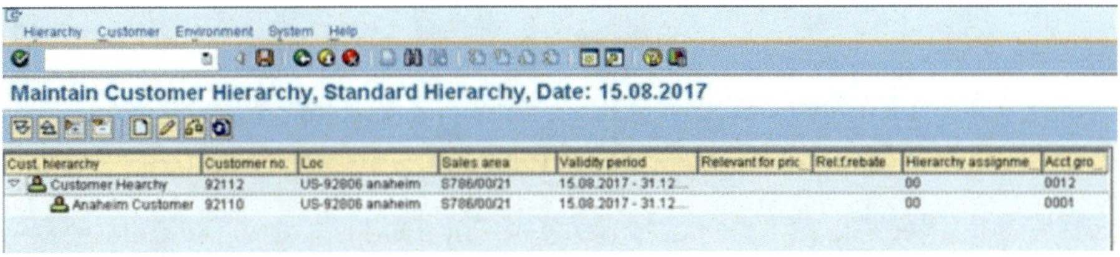

Figure H791

Display Customer hierarchy:

Transaction Code: VDH2N

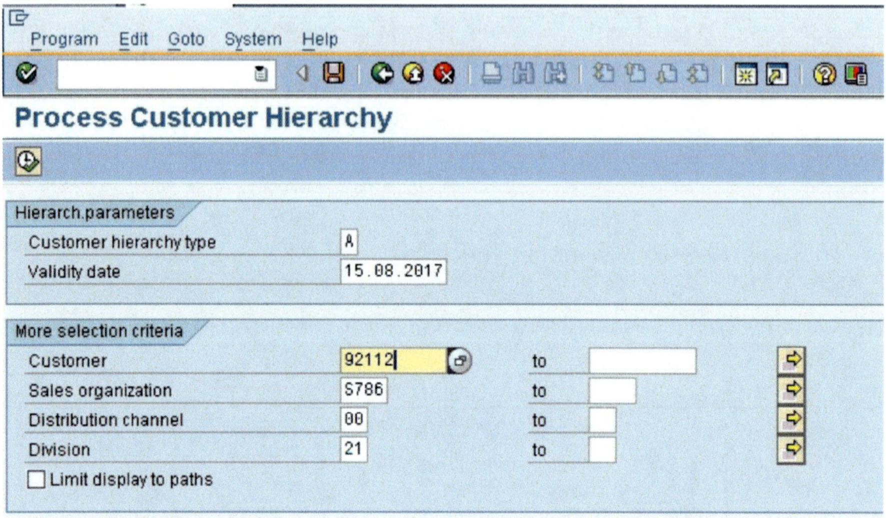

Figure H792

Enter the customer hierarchy type "A", Validity date and customer number as required entries, in more selection criteria please enter the sales area.

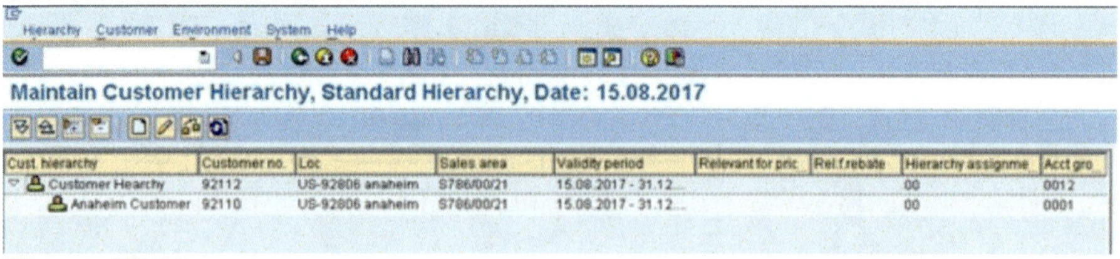

Figure H793

In above screenshot we can review the customer hierarchy

First Field is the name of the customer. The 2nd field is Customer hierarchy customer number. LOC stand for location, and is the address of the customer master

Index:

ABAP, 26
Account Payment, 29
account receivable, 96
Account Receivable, 29
Accrual, 29
Additional customer data, 84
additional partner functions, 65
AR, 29
Automatic credit check, 91
Back, 43
Best Practices, 19
Bill to, 63
buttons and shortcuts, 43
Cancel, 43
Common distribution channel, 65
Common Division, 65
company, 50
Company code, 50
Company Code, 80
Company code data, 57
Company Code Data, 53
company codes, 90
contact person, 75
Credit, 32
Credit check, 91
Credit control, 51
Credit Control area, 90
credit control area., 92
credit control areas, 96
Credit exposure, 90, 92
Credit management, 90
Credit Management, 90
CRM, 36
currency, 90
Currency, 76
Customer credit block, 97
customer hierarchy, 104
Customer hierarchy, 76, 99
Customer master, 53
Customer Master Data, 48
Customer Master Mind Map, 53
Customer Master Partner Functions, 61
customer sales area, 76
Data in SAP, 28
debit, 32
Debit, 32
Delivery priority, 77
Development, 25
Development System, 25
Distribution channels, 52
division, 52
Dynamic credit check, 92
End User, 108
Enter, 43
enterprise structure, 50
Enterprise Structure, 49
ERP, 23
Error, 45
Exit, 45, 46
Export data, 74
External Number Range, 28
financial calculation, 31
Find Next, 43
First Page, 44
General data, 55
General Data, 54
General Ledger Accounting, 31
good receiving, 73
GUI, 36, 38
GUI Installation steps, 36
Hard Error, 46
Industry key, 71
Information, 46

internal number range, 27
IS-Auto, 13
IS-Oil and Gas, 13
IS-Retail, 13
Issue Log, 21
Journal entries, 31
Last Page, 44
Log Off, 43
master data, 49
Master Data, 28
Modules, 17
Multiple Partner Information, 64
New Session, 44
Number Range, 27
One Time Customer, 65
Open New Session, 41
partial delivery, 78
partner function, 79
Payer, 63
Payment transaction, 72
process flow, 30
Production, 25
Production System, 26
Project Issue, 21
Project Risk Management, 22
Quality, 25
Quality System, 25
RECIFW, 30
Sales area, 52, 59
sales organization, 52
SAP easy access, 38
SAP Easy Access Menu, 38
SAP ECC, 37
SAP ERP, 30
SAP GUI, 36
SAP Messages T, 45
Save, 43
Ship to Partner function, 63
Simple credit check, 91
SME, 33
sold to, 62
Success, 45, 46
T-account, 31
T-Account, 31
T-code, 39
T-code bar, 40
Terms of payment, 78
Transaction Code Short Cuts, 41
Transactional Date, 29
Unloading Point, 73
Use case, 30
validity date, 100
Vendor, 71
warning, 45
Warning, 46
Workflow, 29
XD01, 68

ABOUT THE AUTHOR

Certified for IBM. WebSphere. software

SAP® Certified Associate

Syed Awais Rizvi in SAP Specialist/Architect currently working in automotive industry. He has been a strong Project Lead and covered numerous SAP project life cycles. He has experience in SAP Project Management and Implementation. He has worked on upgrade projects, Maintenance projects, template roll-outs and Production Support projects. He has diverse experience in Global implementation of Europe, AIPAC, Middle East and North America from project conception to go-live. He has experience working with Fortune 500 companies. He is SAP SD and SAP Project Management certified.

Connect with him on LinkedIn is at www.linkedin.com/in/syedawaisrizvi you may reach Syed Awais Rizvi via email rrizvir@gmail.com for feedback or query.

Authors Publications

1) Quick SAP Basic Introduction End User Guide: Learn SAP GUI Navigation, Reports, Tips and Tricks with Basic SAP Skills

Published on Feb 2017

2) SAP Sales and Distribution Quick Configuration Guide: Advanced SAP Tips and Tricks with Variant Configuration

Published on May 2015

3) 12 Powerful Leadership and Management Skills: Leadership for Productivity and Project Management

Published on Oct 2016

4) Urdu Beginners Guide: Start Speaking Urdu Phrases with English Pronunciations Learn Urdu Quickly

Published on Jan 2017

5) How to Become Effective Business Analyst Practical Beginners Guide: Real-life Software Requirements and Design Techniques

How to Become
Effective
Business
Analyst
Practical
Beginners Guide
Real-life Software Requirements and Design Techniques

Made in United States
Orlando, FL
05 November 2026

90208300R10067